HAUNTED HEARTS

True Ghostly Love Stories

Barbara Smith

Ghost House Books

The Publisher: Ghost House Books

Distributed by Lone Pine Publishing
10145 – 81 Avenue   1808 B Street NW, Suite 140
Edmonton, AB T6E 1W9   Auburn, WA 98001
Canada   USA

Website: http://www.ghostbooks.net

Library and Archives Canada Cataloguing in Publication

Smith, Barbara, 1947-
    Haunted hearts / Barbara Smith.

ISBN-13: 978-1-894877-77-0
ISBN-10: 1-894877-77-2

    1. Ghosts. 2. Love stories, Canadian (English). 3. Legends. I. Title.

GR580.S669 2005   398.25   C2005-904120-X

Editorial Director: Nancy Foulds
Project Editors: Dawn Loewen, Carol Woo
Production Manager: Gene Longson
Layout & Production: Willa Kung
Cover Design: Gerry Dotto

Photography Credits:
Photo Credits: Every effort has been made to accurately credit photographers. Any errors or omissions should be directed to the publisher for changes in future editions. The photographs in this book are reproduced with the kind permission of the following sources: Destiny Tour Hearses (p. 21); Don Cesar Beach Resort Hotel (p. 8, 11); Girl Scouts of the USA (p. 187, 190); Glenbow Archives (p.180: NA-1406-105); Lyn Inglis (p. 172); Jan Jones (p. 92); Library of Congress (p. 24: HABS, FLA,44-KEY,4-1; p. 33: USZ62-51172; p. 34: DIG-ppmsc-08565; pp. 4-5, p. 39: DIG-ppmsc-08583; p. 63: USZ62-99820; p. 87: USZ62-90327; p. 102: HABS, DC,WASH,8-20; p. 105: USZ62-59758; p. 122: USZ62-45325; p. 161: USZ62-8322); Barbara Smith (p. 48, 211, 214, 217); Carol Woo (p. 50, 89).

We acknowledge the financial support of the Government of Canada through the Book Publishing Industry Development Program (BPIDP) for our publishing activities.

PC: P5

For my grandson Gregory James Trumbley,
who has a heart of gold

Contents

FOREWORD

Love is probably the most haunting of all human emotions. Whether between a woman and a man, a parent and a child, a brother and a sister, even between humans and animals or humans and inanimate objects, love truly forges ties that bind, often forever.

Love ties can be intensely passionate and almost unbearably intimate or simply comforting and quietly ever-present, usually varying over time to blend different mixtures that inflame and becalm us throughout the course of our lives. Those who don't have love search for it endlessly. Those who do have love search for ways to keep what they have. Memories will be relived, anticipations rehearsed, over and over and over again.

Almost inevitably, love thwarted becomes love intensified. Infatuation and enchantment, lust and hate, adoration and revenge, all close cousins often entwined with love, add fuel to love's fires. Only indifference lies outside love's realm and is immune to its influence.

Without love, we wither. With love, our hearts are imbued with a powerful life force—and quite possibly even with a powerful afterlife force.

Barbara Smith has managed to touch on these themes both directly and indirectly in her collection of stories, all crafted in her own uniquely compelling style.

Read on and enjoy!

—Barrie W. Robinson, Ph.D., author of *Love Counts, Gender Roles, Gender in the 1990s, Gigolos and Madames Bountiful* and *Gender in Canada*.

PREFACE

Love might be the only theme as universal as ghosts. After all, who of us·has not been haunted by an affair of the heart? Perhaps that is one of the reasons I found this project absolutely irresistible.

The ghostly love stories presented in *Haunted Hearts* range from ancient folklore to situations that are current and ongoing. The kinds of love described in these tales are equally different. Despite these differences, throughout the collection love remains the motivating factor for the haunting, and as with all of my books, each story has been reported to me as true. Of course, it would be as difficult, and as pointless, to try to convince a skeptic to believe in ghosts as it would be to try to convince someone emotionally paralyzed about the existence of love. It is not my intent to wade into either debate. My only hope is that, as you read this book, you will share the enjoyment I felt while researching, compiling and writing these ghostly love stories.

Collecting and writing the stories in *Haunted Hearts* would not have been nearly as much fun without the help of the following people. Paranormal researcher W. Ritchie Benedict of Calgary, Alberta, has contributed his amazing skills to my work for many years now and this project was no exception. Thank you, Ritchie. Bonnie Robbins of Brandon, Manitoba, also found obscure leads, many of which turned into some fascinating stories. In addition, all of the people associated with "The Birthplace" were extremely helpful, as was Sunny Ricks with the Don CeSar Beach Resort. Allan Levinson, owner of Destiny Tours in Sydney, Australia, has continued his friendly support of my projects, as has Jan

Jones. Ron Myhre of Port Townsend, Washington, Dr. Richard Wiseman of the University of Hertfordshire, Lyn Inglis of Revelstoke, British Columbia, and Sophie Trebaczkiewicz of Edmonton, Alberta, all went out of their way to contribute to this book. I thank you all from the bottom of my heart. And, as he has done for many years now, my dear friend Dr. Barrie W. Robinson contributed his considerable editing and research skills to this project. Thank you, Barrie. Many thanks, too, are owed to my husband, Bob, as well as my daughters, Debbie and Robyn.

Very special thanks to everyone at Ghost House Books whose efforts and expertise make these books possible, most especially Grant Kennedy, Shane Kennedy, Nancy Foulds, Dawn Loewen, Carol Woo, Gene Longson, Willa Kung and Gerry Dotto.

Loved and Loving Phantoms

Staying at the Don CeSar Beach Resort in October could seem like stepping into a glamorous and intriguing historical romance novel, for that is when the luxurious St. Pete Beach, Florida, hotel celebrates its status as a haunted hostelry.

Today, the gorgeous "Pink Palace" is as grand a resort as it was back in 1928, when it was built by Thomas Rowe, an Irish immigrant. According to the official history of the hotel (the source of all quotations in this story), in those early days "the resort reigned as the hot spot for high society." F. Scott Fitzgerald, Clarence Darrow, Lou Gehrig and even Al Capone loved to visit "the Don," and Thomas Rowe loved playing host to such famous and infamous guests. Few knew that Rowe had built the splendid hotel to honor and commemorate a forbidden love.

In the 1890s, when Rowe was a young man living in London, he fell in love with "a dark-eyed beauty" named Lucinda. Her parents did not approve of the union and they forbade the lovers from seeing one another. Apparently not trusting

Thomas Rowe loved his hotel almost as much as he loved Lucinda.

the couple to respect that decree, Lucinda's mother and father banished their daughter to the countryside. Heartbroken, Thomas Rowe moved to America.

By the time Rowe made his fortune dealing in Florida real estate, his beloved young Lucinda had died. Rowe set about building a tribute to his lost love, "the pink castle they had always dreamed of." The reality of such emotionally laden dreams is never inexpensive, and construction of the hotel ran 300 percent over budget. Despite its cost, the forbidden love between Rowe and Lucinda was at last suitably memorialized—right down to the courtyard and fountain that were replicas of the spot where the two had courted.

Rowe and his legacy of love prospered for a dozen years. Then one day in 1940, as he walked across the lobby of his beloved Don CeSar hotel, Thomas Rowe collapsed and died of a heart attack.

Fortunately, he had written a will in which he bequeathed his "Pink Palace" to his "loyal family of employees." Unfortunately, Thomas Rowe had never signed that will. A woman Rowe had briefly been married to, but had been estranged from for 30 years, became the hotel's reluctant heir.

The former Mrs. Rowe apparently had little desire or ability to maintain the hotel as a monument to lost love. The hotel rather quickly lost its luster and, within three years of Rowe's death, the building and grounds were sold to the U.S. Army. They were turned first into a convalescent center for shell-shocked World War II veterans and later into a Veterans Administration office. The VA quit the location in the mid-1960s when it could no longer afford the upkeep. The downward spiral continued as "the abandoned building became a graffiti canvas, doomed for the wrecking ball."

Such a romantic setting should be home to a love story—and it is.

The travesty of abuse and neglect that had befallen the grand old edifice was finally arrested in 1973, when a group of concerned citizens found a buyer for the place. From that day on, there has been no looking back. The Don CeSar Beach Resort, as the "Pink Palace" is now officially known, is more opulent than ever. It boasts nearly 300 luxuriously appointed guest rooms, a full-service Beach Club and Spa, a four-star dining room and two swimming pools.

Perhaps the most important restorations have been to the hotel's lobby—the hotel's haunted lobby—for that is where many people have seen Rowe's image. The former owner is easily recognizable in his summer suit and Panama hat. He is said to be "casting a watchful presence over the Don and welcoming guests."

Legend has it that, at the moment of Thomas Rowe's death in 1940, the spirit of his beloved Lucinda flew to his side. His spirit is also often seen walking hand-in-hand along the shoreline near the hotel with a woman whom witnesses describe as a dark-haired beauty.

No wonder the hotel's owners celebrate the Don CeSar's ghosts. It would be difficult to conceive of a more hauntingly romantic tale!

Bridge Across Time

The man's full name has been lost in the mists of time. Today, we know only that his last name was Brown, and that he was a cad.

Picture an annual church picnic in a small Ohio town, circa the 1890s. To no one's surprise, Enos Kay, a young man of 20, has escorted the lovely Alvira to the get-together. Enos was an ambitious and determined young man. He hesitated to ask for Alvira's hand in marriage until he had enough money to ensure that on their wedding day he would carry her over the threshold of a properly constructed home.

Perhaps he never bothered to explain his plans to Alvira, or perhaps she grew tired of waiting for Enos to ask for her hand. Whichever was the case, Alvira arrived at the church picnic that day with Enos, but left arm-in-arm with Brown. The handsome, smooth-talking interloper had charmed his way into Alvira's heart. Just two days later, shock waves rippled through the town and the gossips' tongues wagged. Mr. Kay's intended had eloped with Mr. Brown.

Poor Enos was completely overwhelmed with grief. Just a few days later, he penned a long, rambling rant expressing his hurt and anger. It was his suicide note. Before signing his name to the missive, Enos vowed that having lost the love of his life he would, in death, exact his revenge. The ink on that note was barely dry when the young man placed it under a rock on the railing of the old covered wooden bridge that crossed the town's river.

With that, the heartbroken man jumped to his death.

Just days later, a young couple from the town stopped on the bridge, hoping that its shadows would provide privacy for their romantic intentions. As the pair entered the darkened tunnel, the horse pulling their buggy reared up in alarm. No matter how hard he tried, the driver could not calm his usually placid and obedient horse. It didn't take long for the two lovers to realize that they were not going to have the tender moment they'd hoped for.

Only when the man ordered his horse to walk ahead did the animal finally calm down. By the time the young lovers found their way back to town, they had decided not to say anything to anyone about their strange experience. They felt it would be easy for all but the most dull-witted to guess why they had gone to the bridge in the first place, and that would only reflect badly upon them.

A few days later, at dusk one evening, another pair of lovers sought out the sanctuary of the covered bridge. As soon as the horse had pulled their buggy under cover of the bridge, the poor animal became almost enraged. It too reared up on its hind legs, whinnying in piteous anxiety. Frightened by the strange turn of events, the couple decided to flee from the darkened place as soon as their horse calmed down enough to obey an order. As they fled, they vowed never to go near it again—even the noise of their horse's hooves galloping across the floor of the wooden structure could not cover the sounds of sinister cackling laughter echoing from the bridge. Once they were safely away from the eerie bridge, the pair turned to look back at it. A grey ball of mist, about the height and size of a man, swirled around just at the rail. For a moment, the mist thickened and the frightened couple was sure they saw a pair of red, beady eyes staring out at them from the dark vapors.

It wasn't long before most of the young couples in town had been frightened by an inexplicable something on the bridge, and soon the place had a well-deserved reputation for being haunted. Over the years leading to the early 20th century, reports of ghostly encounters on that bridge remained consistent. If a horse-drawn buggy was just passing through, neither the horse nor the people were disturbed. If the people stopped to share a bit of romance, they were virtually guaranteed to have a frightening encounter with the jilted ghost of Enos Kay.

And what of the fickle Alvira and the womanizing Brown? Did they at least make a success of the hastily arranged escape that caused such fatal and haunting results? No one knows the answers to those questions.

Today, that haunted old bridge is only a memory in the annals of the town, and it is generally presumed that Enos Kay's tortured spirit finally found its eternal rest.

The Lovely Ladies

Lots of people will tell you that they "love" their cars, but can cars love people? A car is just a car, isn't it? Well, not always, apparently.

Many years ago there was a television situation comedy called *My Mother the Car,* based on the premise that a man's rather fussy, but kind and loving, mother had been reincarnated as a car. You might think that sort of thing is pretty far-fetched and not possible in real life, but there *are* tales of haunted vehicles. Some of those stories are utterly delightful, as is the one about two cars in Sydney, New South Wales, Australia.

These cars, both of them hearses, transport guests on Weird Sydney Ghost and History Tours, and by happiest coincidence for our purposes here, both of the touring "ladies" have intriguing love stories associated with them. Their owner, Allan, the Hearse Whisperer and owner of Destiny Tours, says that, while he is extremely fond and proud of both cars, "Elvira" is the one he's "more bonded" with. He explained, "I bought her in 1999 when I seemed to have been inexplicably drawn to the vehicle and felt it was my destiny to own her. At the time, I bought her just as a hobby car. She was still a hearse and I did not realize that 12 months later she would be part of my new exciting business venture."

Since then, Allan and Elvira have established a close relationship. "As I work nearly every night with the car, I am quite in tune with her various ways. She has very strong energies at the front, which many other people can also feel. I would never sell the car," he said. "In fact, I have her tattooed on my upper arm."

But Allan isn't the only man in Elvira's life. There's also the ghost who haunts her. Over the years, many people have felt the spirit's presence, and psychic Debbie Malone has validated those feelings. In a letter to Allan, Debbie stated, "I have traveled in Elvira and can definitely confirm a presence in the seat directly behind the driver's. I feel this presence is a man in a black suit with a white shirt, similar to what an undertaker would wear. He has glasses and sometimes wears a hat."

Debbie was even able to identify the spirit by name: Tom. She went on to explain that Tom "means no harm to anyone, he just loves to travel in the car. I have also noticed on occasions that, if anyone is mocking Tom's presence, that person suddenly develops a feeling of nausea and needs to change seats immediately."

Despite Tom's unpleasant way of straightening out those who are not taking his ghostly existence seriously, Debbie acknowledged that "Elvira has a feeling of peace about her" and that Tom is generally a friendly spirit. Judging from what else Allan has to say about Elvira's resident phantom, some people would even say that Tom is too friendly.

Allan explained that, occasionally, as his passengers are enjoying their tour through the haunted streets of Sydney, some of the women in the car have actually had more fun than they bargained for. "Lately, some women have admitted to becoming sexually aroused on the tour," Allan began. Whenever this anomaly occurs, the women are sitting "in the seat behind the driver's seat, where Tom our resident spirit sits." None of the women has ever been able to explain why this was happening to her.

Tom's influence isn't always quite so directly physical. "There have been several romances based around the hearses," Allan said. "Once a young guy proposed to a girl on the tour, so she got back into the car after a regularly scheduled break wearing an engagement ring. I've also heard that a couple met on the tour."

Elvira's "older sister" is "Morticia," a rare 1962 Cadillac hearse/ambulance combination. "She's one of only 28 ever made," Allan said. "Often in American small towns, the local funeral director also supplied the ambulance service for the community." Allan bought Morticia in 2001 and "lovingly restored her mechanically and gave her a complete interior makeover" before putting her on the road in 2002 as an important addition to the Weird Sydney Ghost and History Tours.

Morticia is at least as haunted as Elvira is. Not every person requiring an ambulance lived through their illness and so occasionally people did die as they rode in Morticia. Today, passengers with a sensitive nature will sometimes experience lower abdominal pains at some point during a tour. Allan explained that "psychics have investigated Morticia and say that a young girl died of a burst appendix in the car and the child's spirit is still trapped [here]."

Because the presence of a ghost can attract other supernatural activity, the soul of the little girl often has company as Morticia is driven around to the various haunted places visited on the tour of Sydney. Sometimes, for no earthly reason, passengers' cameras will temporarily malfunction; other times, the fragrance of roses suddenly permeates the air in the car. Passengers have clearly seen the shadows of three people when only two living beings were present. Psychics have detected the specter of a well-dressed man about 60 years of age. They say that he died of chest problems in the car. It is that spirit, no doubt, who causes some passengers to experience discomfort in the chest. It happens in only one particular area of Morticia, and once the passenger moves to another seat, he or she inevitably feels well again.

Morticia has played a direct role in an utterly charming love story. Allan explained, "This is the love story of a beautiful vehicle which happens to be a hearse named Morticia and a devoted lady named Caroline. It all started on Australia Day [January 26], 2003." Allan was exhibiting Morticia at a car show that day.

"A tall, striking-looking lady walked over to admire Morticia. We got talking and I ended up giving her a lift home after the show. Caroline's background was in the funeral industry and she was experienced in all facets of the field including embalming, makeup of the deceased and other related activities. Caroline was very interested in my Weird Sydney Ghost and History Tours, so I invited her along one night as my guest. Not only did Caroline love Morticia, with the car's beautiful lines and snow leopard interior, but she also loved the whole concept of an offbeat tour in a hearse."

It only made sense for Allan to hire Caroline to be a driver/tour guide for Destiny Tours. Since then, Caroline has become a valued employee, and with her dramatic appearance, including the 19 bat tattoos on her arms, she "certainly looks the part of a hearse tour driver." Some nights it seems that she attracts almost as much attention as Morticia herself does.

"Customers always give excellent feedback and Caroline enjoys her job very much, so much so that it is hard to get her away from the car! As a result, people ask her if it is her car, to which she replies, 'It is my car, but Allan owns it.'"

Morticia seems to share Caroline's sentiment. One day when the driver was not yet at work, a female passenger who was clearly psychically sensitive, but not at all familiar with Morticia or her background, "put her head in the front cabin section of Morticia and straightaway said the name 'Caroline.'"

Recently Caroline was on holidays in New Zealand. Allan missed his stellar employee, but Morticia also reacted to the young woman's absence. Allan recalled, "The night Caroline left, I was driving Morticia home after a tour. When I was about five miles from home, Morticia came to a stop. Her automatic transmission had died and I had to have her towed to a repairer. In hindsight, I think Morticia waited for that moment to break down because she didn't want to break down for Caroline."

Allan's theory might be correct, because Morticia was ready for the road again on the day Caroline returned from holidays. That evening, the two striking ladies were happily reunited!

Because of Morticia's previous incarnation as a combination ambulance and hearse, as Allan reiterated, "people were unfortunately suffering and dying in there, and in fact did die in there. Many people can still feel the sad energies of the car and can be affected by all sorts of pains whilst in and around the car. But Caroline's so bonded to Morticia and shows so much love and affection to it that she is able to calm down the energies so that she is not so much affected." Or maybe Morticia calms down the energies herself because she loves Caroline so much that she doesn't want her friend and driver to suffer.

Little did anyone suspect that Morticia would find a way to thank Caroline for all the tender loving care and kindness the young woman bestows upon the vehicle. Allan explained that, when she is not touring, Morticia stays at a car park in

It was only fitting that Morticia be chosen as the wedding car. After all, her spirit ensured that the bride and groom would meet!

the Kings Cross district of Sydney. A security company keeps its cars in the same garage.

"About a year ago, Caroline met one of the security guards there, a man named Paul. The two are due to be married next week and, of course, I will be driving the happy couple to their wedding in Morticia."

Quite a series of "coincidences" led the couple to the altar. First of all, Morticia was the reason Allan met Caroline, "who is without a doubt the best employee one could hope for as well as a good friend who will help out at any time with anything." Then, working for Allan and driving the beautiful hearse led Caroline to meet Paul, her future husband. "Caroline is expecting a baby with Paul and is the happiest person at the moment."

Perhaps not to be outdone by Morticia, her "sister" Elvira may soon have a love story of her own to tell. Without revealing too much, Allan candidly acknowledged that, through Elvira's spirit, he has met his own "perfect match," but cautioned that we won't know the "hopefully happy ending to the story" for a while.

These beautiful, haunted, loving and well-loved hearses are clearly not through playing Cupid yet!

Love So Gruesome

Occasionally, the apparition of a young woman is seen drifting about the lively community of Key West, Florida. Many people who have seen the ghost believe it is the spirit of Elena Hoyos, whose story is virtually guaranteed to haunt you for a very long time.

Elena was born in 1909 to a family made financially comfortable by her father's employment in the lucrative cigar-manufacturing business. By the time she was a teenager in the mid-1920s, carefree Elena had become the belle of many a local ball. With a flower pinned in her jet-black hair, she often danced the night away.

Sadly, Elena's happy and untroubled days were numbered. The aftermath of World War I had a devastating impact on the cigar business, and her father's income gradually dwindled to the point that he could no longer provide his family with the luxuries they'd become accustomed to. Those financial setbacks paled compared with the problem that next assaulted the family—tuberculosis. The disease spread like wildfire through the same cigar factory that had previously provided the Hoyoses with an enviable standard of living.

Soon, Elena was an orphan with a worrisome, lingering cough in the midst of a tuberculosis epidemic. Finally, when she could not bear the dreaded disease's debilitating cough any longer, the dangerously ill young woman went to the hospital in Key West.

The "doctor" who attended to Elena was a man who variously called himself either Count Von Cosel or Dr. Carl (or Karl) Tanzler. A recent German immigrant, the man maintained that in addition to his medical degree, he had eight

Key West, Florida was home to one of the strangest love stories the world has ever known.

other degrees—all supposedly granted by European universities. A retrospective examination of the situation reveals that, although each of Von Cosel's titles and degrees was likely a product of his imagination, he did apparently work hard to ease his patients' suffering.

The "doctor" was in his early 50s the day that the ailing 21-year-old Elena Hoyos walked into the hospital seeking medical attention. She instantly and unwittingly stole the middle-aged man's heart. In a vain attempt to cheat death, Elena cooperated with Von Cosel as he fought to save her life. Their efforts were defeated, and Elena Hoyos died on October 22, 1931, at the age of 22. Von Cosel was utterly heartbroken. He had wished to marry Elena and be with her forever. Now those wishes had been irrevocably destroyed.

For most love stories, that would have been the tragic end to the story. But most love stories don't feature a man as mentally unstable and obsessively determined as Von Cosel. Day after day, the "doctor" went to Elena's grave in the Key West cemetery. He took her flowers and stayed to visit with her while she, he reported, sang love songs to him. Before long, the man maintained, she asked him to take her home with him.

He did.

For more than seven years, Von Cosel lived with the woman's corpse, attempting all the while to bring her back to life. In his demented mind he did revive her and went so far as to attest that, whenever she expressed a desire to get up, he advised her just to lie there and rest. This ghoulish situation might have gone on even longer had it not been for Elena's sister, who became suspicious regarding the whereabouts of her deceased sister's remains. The woman was overwhelmed when the coroner informed her that the "wax dummy" she had found on Von Cosel's premises was actually the pre-served body of her long-dead sister.

Authorities discovered that, by using the medical knowl-edge he had gained from his years working in the local hospi-tal, and a constant supply of perfume to counteract the stench, the man had managed to slow the decay of Elena's body. He even went so far as to place glass eyes in the corpse's empty eye sockets! The gruesome remains, and Von Cosel himself, were immediately taken into custody.

Amazingly, the count was soon released. His crime—grave robbery—had exceeded the statute of limitations and, per-haps even more incredibly, he was deemed to be sane.

The indignities to the poor beleaguered body of Elena Hoyos were not yet over. It was paraded through the town for all to see—even schoolchildren were given a partial holiday from classes to line the streets and catch a glimpse of the gruesome oddity. Eventually, the woman's body was laid to rest. It was decided that the poor soul had a better chance of finally resting in peace if the site was kept a secret and the deed was done in the dark of night. After all, no one wanted to think about what might happen if the "doctor" knew where his beloved lay and found himself a shovel!

In 1952, Carl Tanzler, the "Count Von Cosel," died in his home at Zephyrhills, Florida. He was found alone, slumped over a life-sized mannequin of his beloved Elena Hoyos as it lay in a casket, dressed in a wedding gown.

No wonder the poor young soul is said to haunt the area where she lived and died and then lived again—at least in the mind of her mad count.

House Haunted by Unfulfilled Love

In days gone by, stories of haunted houses sometimes made the newspaper. On July 28, 1928, for instance, the now-defunct *Edmonton Bulletin* in Alberta, Canada, carried the following report:

STRANGE RAPS IN EMPTY HOUSE
Jilted Bride Never Forgot
Unfaithful Lover in Edmonton

Mysterious knockings in an empty house are intriguing the residents of Bush Hill Park, Edmonton, Alberta.

The story connected with this deserted home is reminiscent of Satis House in Dickens' *Great Expectations*, in which the jilted Miss Havisham lived, wearing her wedding dress.

Exactly two years ago, Miss McCloy, the last occupant, was found dead in the house; she had died some weeks before her body was discovered, but there were no signs of foul play.

No relatives could be traced. The keys are held by the coroner's officer and Miss McCloy's jewels and investments—totaling over 1,000 Pounds Sterling—are held by the Treasury.

It is said that Miss McCloy—like Miss Havisham—received on the morning of her wedding day a letter from her lover saying that he had changed his mind, and was going abroad. She was broken-hearted but could not, apparently, stifle her love.

Roses, the favourite flower of her faithless lover, were the only blooms she would grow in her garden; his photograph was ever on her wall and it is believed that she left him all her property.

He cannot be found. But neighbours say that a man driving a car has recently visited the house.

And the strange rappings are said to come from the wall on which his photograph used to hang.

His Determination Didn't Die

Colorado mining camps of the 1860s were rough-and-tumble places. A head count at any camp would show that women were in short supply; because of this imbalance, the living was less than genteel. That state of affairs might not seem conducive to producing a ghost story with a romantic bent, but at one camp, the Buckskin Joe Mining Camp, that is exactly what happened. Better still, this tale is even rather humorous.

For the most part, men who populated the mining camps had traveled great distances and undergone terrible hardships to get there. Discovering gold—lots of it—was what was important to these men, not living a refined or dignified life while in camp. As a result, sometimes even the dying wasn't very sophisticated.

The exact date has been forgotten, but sometime in 1863 a man by the name of J. Dawson Hidgepath arrived at the Buckskin Joe Mining Camp. No one asked where Hidgepath had come from. No one *ever* asked that of any of the miners. If a man chose not to talk, then his silence was respected. There was an unwritten code of respect for another person's right to privacy, even if amenities and culture around the camp were in short supply.

Unfortunately, Hidgepath either wasn't aware of that code or chose to ignore it. He asked lots of questions—or rather the same question—to lots of people, all of them the wrong people. You see, J. Dawson didn't just want gold, he wanted a wife, too, and so he asked every woman in the camp for her hand in marriage. But all the women were already married—to Hidgepath's miner colleagues! Needless to say, the husbands weren't too pleased to hear that the newcomer had been so forthcoming!

One angry husband punched J. Dawson Hidgepath, and another shot at him, but nothing stopped the romantic miner's proposals.

Today, it's tough to know whether all parts of this tale are true or not, but the story goes that on a beautiful day in July 1865, young Mr. Hidgepath decided to take a walk. While on that walk, he lost his footing and fell down the side of a hill. By the time he reached the bottom of that hill, J. Dawson Hidgepath was dead.

No version of this legend implicates any of the angry husbands at the Buckskin Joe Mining Camp as being in any way responsible for the death. It would seem that the men were innocent, and that Hidgepath had merely been as unlucky on a walk as he had been in love.

It turns out that Hidgepath was just as determined a fellow in death as he was in life. It wasn't long after his earthly remains had been buried in Buckskin Cemetery that the women of the camp began having visitations from a ghost with marriage on his mind—the ghost of J. Dawson Hidgepath, of course.

After the specter had paid a spooky call on two local women and frightened them half to death, their husbands decided to dig up Hidgepath's remains and rebury him—deeper this time. But a silly thing like a bit of extra depth apparently wasn't enough to stop a wraith with a will to wed. The next day, the local seamstress fainted dead away when she saw Hidgepath's spirit walk into her shop. Presumably he wasn't looking just for a new suit to be reburied in. More likely, he was in search of a wedding suit and a bride to match.

That evening, as soon as they were finished work, the miners went to the graveyard and stacked many huge, heavy boulders on top of J. Dawson's grave. This haunting simply had to stop.

But it didn't.

Hidgepath's soul would simply not rest in unmarried peace. When his ghost approached the mayor's wife, the matter became official. His Lordship ordered that this nonsense must cease immediately. He organized a posse of the best miners in the camp and together they dug their way down, again, until they reached Hidgepath's coffin. They opened the rough wooden box and tilted it so that the contents would fall into a big sack they'd brought with them for that purpose. Their plan was to ride to the closest center, which was Leadville, Colorado, and leave the would-be lover's corpse there for the city folk to deal with. But that meant they'd have to haul the heavy, cumbersome, and undoubtedly smelly sack over the mountains. By that time, it was getting late in the day and their wives would be wondering what was keeping them.

One of the men came up with a devilishly clever shortcut to solving the problem. Moments later, J. Dawson Hidgepath's earthly remains had been dumped into the bowels (pardon the pun) of an outhouse! Surely *that* would keep the ghost away from their wives, they said, slapping one another on the back in celebration of their cleverness.

And their plan worked! At least to some degree. No one ever saw the ghost of J. Dawson Hidgepath again. Unfortunately, the ladies still heard from the deceased Romeo regularly because, every time one of them visited that outhouse, a ghostly voice would bellow up and ask for her hand in marriage.

Royal Revenants

Arabella was born a princess. She married and became a Lady; died and became a lovelorn ghost.

The year was 1575 and Elizabeth Cavendish was overjoyed with the excitement of being a new mother. Her newborn was a girl and as beautiful a child as any mother could hope for. She named the infant Arabella. But neither the girl's beauty nor her mother's great love for her were enough to protect her from tragedy.

As a descendant of King Henry VIII, Arabella stood second in line for the English throne after her cousin, King James VI of Scotland. In 1603, James succeeded Queen Elizabeth I and became James I of England. He became obsessed with the fear that Arabella would one day murder him in order to take over the throne.

But by then the lovely woman's thoughts could not have been farther from the possibility of becoming queen. You see, Arabella had fallen in love. The object of her affections was the dashing and handsome Sir William Seymour, and he was equally smitten. A wedding, it seemed, was imminent.

This news drove the paranoid King James into a panic. He was convinced that as soon as Sir William and Arabella married, the couple would plot to kill him, so he forbade them from seeing one another. When they disobeyed, the king ordered his guards to arrest them both and lock them away.

By the time they were hunted down and caught, in 1610, the couple had secretly married. When he uncovered the deception, King James was furious. He had Sir William locked away in the dreaded Tower of London, while Arabella was kept at Lambeth Palace, London.

The obsessive King James I locked the lovely Arabella at Lambeth Palace.

The couple's friends and family were shocked and frightened at James' terrible cruelty. The bravest of those allies were able to help the imprisoned couple communicate with one another, and the lovers eventually devised a plan to escape from their cells and flee the country. But Lady Arabella was captured almost immediately. Furious with her continuing disobedience, King James locked the lovesick woman away again. In 1615, tragedy struck: Arabella died, some say of a broken heart.

William was more fortunate. His escape was successful and permanent. He went on to live a long life as the Marquess of Hertford, not joining his true love in the afterlife until 1660. Almost immediately after his death, people began to see a pair of misty images occasionally strolling

A pair of misty apparitions have been seen wandering the halls of Lambeth Palace.

hand in hand on the grounds of Lambeth Palace. Sightings of the reunited ghostly lovers continued for hundreds of years. One of the most detailed reports was documented in 1864.

Emma Petrie, a seamstress at Lambeth Palace, knew nothing of this tragic tale. One autumn day in 1864, when she was making her way along a palace corridor, she saw another woman approaching her. As the two neared one another, the seamstress noted the other woman's regal beauty as well as her heart-wrenchingly sorrowful expression. But it was the lady's decidedly old-fashioned dress that really caught Emma's eye.

The seamstress stood respectfully to the side of the hallway to let the strangely dressed, sad-looking soul pass, and, as she did, a cloud of icy air filled the space between the two. As the image made its way down the hall, Emma stood paralyzed, not by cold but rather by fear. She knew that the sight she beheld was not natural—the oddly dressed, elegant vision could not be from this world. It had to be supernatural because it did not walk, it floated along a few inches above the floor.

Emma struggled to control the panic she could feel rising in her throat. For long moments, the seamstress stood staring down the now-empty corridor. By the time her rapidly beating heart had almost returned to normal, Emma was trying to tell herself that she'd imagined the entire bizarre scene. Unfortunately, later that day, she was treated to a second glimpse into the world beyond. This time she watched in awe as the same ice-cold image glided through a closed door and out of sight.

Badly shaken, the seamstress tried once more to get on with her duties. By the time Emma saw the apparition for a third time that day, she wondered if she should report the sightings. But to whom, and what could she say? She could certainly not say that she had seen a ghost walking about the palace!

That evening, near the end of her working day, the seamstress saw the image one last time. On this occasion, the ghost was outside on the palace grounds. Moments later, the apparition was joined by another entity—a handsome young man in 17th-century attire. The two embraced briefly and joined hands before disappearing from sight.

The next day, in desperation and fearing that she was losing her mind, Emma Petrie confided in another palace worker. It was only then that she learned the story of the lovers' reunited spirits that had haunted Lambeth Palace and its grounds for more than two centuries.

Perhaps they seek each other still.

She Loved and Lost

The intricate maze on the grounds of England's Hampton Court Palace, located on the Thames River about 15 miles southwest of downtown London, is famous worldwide. Maze aficionados travel from all over to see and explore the hedgerow labyrinth. Other visitors to the enormous and exquisite palace grounds skirt that area, claiming they are uncomfortable with the eerie way a maze can disorient a person and affect their powers of reason. It would be interesting to know if those folks also avoid certain places inside the palace. Surely the shrieks that occasionally echo in the Haunted Gallery would be even more disorienting and challenging to their powers of reason—especially if the witnesses knew that those pathetic cries were the desperate pleas of a woman executed more than 450 years ago!

King Henry VIII ruled England from 1509 to 1547. He remains famous, or infamous, on a number of counts but is probably best known for having been married six times. Henry was, to phrase it politely, fickle in matters of the heart, though he was completely consistent in being aware of his responsibility to produce a male heir. It was incorrectly believed at that time that the sex of a newborn was determined by the mother. When Henry's first wife, Catherine of Aragon, failed to produce a living heir, the king apparently felt he had no choice but to replace Catherine with a wife who would help him fulfill his royal obligation.

After making the necessary changes in the country's laws, King Henry VIII divorced Catherine of Aragon and married Anne Boleyn. Anne produced a daughter and a stillborn son. Her punishment was execution for an alleged act of adultery, which left Henry single again and free to marry Jane Seymour (great-grandaunt of Sir William in the previous story). Jane produced a son, Edward, but the boy was not healthy and fears arose that he would not live for long. Shortly after the baby's birth, Jane Seymour died and Edward was sent away to live with relatives.

The determined King Henry remarried. When Anne of Cleves, his fourth wife, also failed to produce the desired heir, he divorced her.

During the summer of 1540, Henry married yet again but neither the marriage nor Katherine Howard, the king's new bride, were long-lived. Relatives of sickly Edward were apparently afraid that Katherine might produce a healthier male heir, so they hatched a plot to convince Henry that his wife had committed adultery with a man named Thomas Culpepper. When Henry heard the news of his wife's alleged unfaithfulness, he immediately ordered that she be charged with, and found guilty of, treasonous adultery.

Katherine was placed under house arrest—the "house" being Hampton Court Palace, a magnificent structure with immense grounds and almost 300 rooms. Here she was to await the executioner, who would take her to the dreaded Tower of London. Upon hearing that Henry was about to attend Mass in the Royal Chapel at the Palace, the desperate Katherine managed to elude her guards. She dashed down the gallery leading to the Royal Chapel, hoping to plead for her life. Alas, just as she began to knock on the chapel door, the guards recaptured her and dragged the terrified woman kicking and shrieking back along the gallery to her prison.

Two days later, on February 13, 1542, Katherine Howard stood on a scaffold at the Tower of London. She uttered a brief speech admitting that she had indeed loved Thomas Culpepper, but denying ever having committed adultery. Sadly, her words did her no good, and seconds later the woman's short life was over. She had truly lost her head over love.

The story of her haunted heart had just begun, because Katherine's spirit has haunted Hampton Court Palace ever since.

A book published as early as 1857 tells of a female image dressed in white seen drifting down the gallery toward the Royal Chapel. Moments after reaching the door, the vision, with her dress now in tatters and screaming in despair, moves back from where she came. This ghostly form, believed to be that of Katherine, has returned to that area of the palace so often that the walkway has become known as the Haunted Gallery.

In the 1930s, a guard reported seeing a disembodied hand knocking on the chapel door. Later, he described the bizarre sight in detail, including a ring that the hand wore. He had described a ring known to have been Katherine Howard's.

Because of Katherine's ghost and many others, Hampton Court Palace has become known as "one of the most haunted places in England," according to Dr. Richard Wiseman, professor of psychology at the University of Hertfordshire in England.

In the spring of 2000, Dr. Wiseman assembled a team of researchers and began an investigation that included the Haunted Gallery at Hampton Court Palace. His scholarly inquiry into the phenomenon was arranged after two women, who were strangers to one another, both fainted in exactly the same spot while taking part in two separate tours. The women both reported that just before they lost consciousness they felt as though they had been punched.

Hampton Court Palace is known to be one of the most haunted places in England.

Dr. Wiseman planned an experiment. The Hampton Court research involved three components. First, a member of the palace staff with the official title of "warder" (security guard) compiled a list of all hauntings in the gallery and indicated their precise location within the walkway. From this information, Professor Wiseman was able to map the gallery, marking "haunted" and unhaunted or "control" areas.

Second, researchers set up instruments to detect changes in the electromagnetic activity at various points in the 40-foot-long gallery. The team placing those instruments had no idea which areas were "haunted" and which were not.

Finally, members of the public visiting the gallery area were asked to volunteer to participate in the study by filling out questionnaires about their experiences as they strolled through the walkway. While some of the participants knew about the stories of hauntings at the palace, others did not. It is intriguing to note that such prior knowledge did not seem to influence the experiences of the participants during the course of the study.

Useful information came from 163 males and 299 females. Approximately half of these 462 people reported a total of 189 "unusual experiences," and 110 people were willing to link their "unusual experience" to the possibility of a ghost.

After the data had been collected, Dr. Wiseman's researchers compared the volunteers' experiences to the floor plan mapped out by the warder of Hampton Court Palace. The researchers discovered that the "unusual experiences" (dizziness, headaches, sickness, shortness of breath, some form of "force," a foul odor, a sense of presence and intense emotional feelings) reported by members of the public were not randomly distributed across all areas of the gallery. They were much more likely to have occurred in the "haunted" areas of the gallery than in the unhaunted or "control" areas.

When the researchers compared the floor plan of previous hauntings to the results of the technical measurements taken, they discovered that the recording instruments had measured significantly higher electromagnetic fluctuations in the "haunted" areas than in the "control" areas. Something was apparently disturbing the force field where the volunteers reported "unusual experiences."

People who know ghost lore are familiar with the theory that a sudden death or even an awareness of an impending death can leave an emotional residue that some people can detect. Dr. Wiseman's experiment seems to indicate that this residue can also be detected by scientific recording devices.

As thought-provoking as the scholarly research is, the various sightings of Katherine will remain the most dramatic proof of the heart-wrenching tragedy and the haunting it caused. If Katherine Howard did indeed commit a crime against king and country, it was perhaps the crime of loving unwisely. Of course, the same charge could be leveled against King Henry VIII.

Lady Louisa Lingers

Just less than 90 miles west of Hampton Court in Warminster, near Bath, England, a hauntingly similar situation exists. The 425-year-long history of Longleat House almost ensures that the palatial residence has its fair share of specters. And that history doesn't let us down. Probably the most famous ghost in the enormous home is that of Lady Louisa Carteret.

Louisa came to live at Longleat after marrying Thomas, the second Viscount of Weymouth, on July 3, 1733. Descriptions of the personalities of Louisa and Thomas make the pairing somewhat of a puzzle because she was apparently as sweet-tempered as he was miserable. The differences in their dispositions might have indirectly led to tragedy, for it seems that when Louisa married the viscount she brought one of her favorite servants with her—a young footman. Whether or not there was ever anything improper about the lady's relationship with her employee, Thomas was clearly threatened by the other man's presence in his wife's life. The viscount dealt with the matter in a swift and permanent manner—he killed the footman and buried the incriminating evidence beneath the basement floor at Longleat. Then, to account for the man's sudden disappearance, the murderer announced that the footman had given notice that he wished to quit his job and permanently leave the area.

Lady Louisa was suspicious and immediately began to search her palatial new home. She never found any evidence of her husband's dastardly deed, but her search was cut short by her own death during childbirth not long after. The woman's body was barely cold in its grave when members of the Longleat household staff began to see her image in a corridor, always wearing a green dress, still searching for her loyal servant who had so mysteriously gone missing.

Some suspect that Thomas also saw his wife's apparition and was terrified at the encounter, perhaps afraid that his deadly deed had come back to haunt him. What is known for certain is that he moved away from Longleat not long after Louisa's death. Despite the viscount's flight from the ghost, Lady Louisa Carteret's haunting of that one particular corridor soon became an accepted feature of the elegant residence.

In the mid-1960s, workers preparing to install central heating at haunted Longleat House made a grisly discovery when they were digging in the basement. Under the stone floor lay the skeleton of a man—still wearing fragments of clothing characteristic of the early to mid-1700s, when Lady Louisa's footman "disappeared." Not wanting unpleasant attention drawn to the house, the remains were quietly reburied in a nearby cemetery.

The attempt at secrecy was probably not altogether successful. Around that time, Lady Louisa's ghost received renewed attention from the media in the form of an American film crew visiting the palace. Their cameras picked up a strange luminous orb moving along the corridor, following the route where Lady Louisa's spirit had so often been seen. Despite investigation by skilled technicians, no earthly explanation was ever found for the anomalous light.

In addition, microphones used during the filming frequently stopped working for no apparent reason, and the overall quality of the resulting footage was surprisingly poor. While these quirks might have surprised the camera crew, ghost hunters would just nod their heads, recognizing such annoyances as commonly accepted signs of a haunting.

Mysterious "Flavours" of Love

When Sophie and her partners bought a restaurant on Whyte Avenue in the Old Strathcona district of Edmonton, Alberta, Canada, they had no reason to expect the unexpected. They had successfully operated restaurants for nearly 20 years and were familiar with the specific challenges and rewards of running a business in this unique area. Although the partners all anticipated a lot of hard work ahead of them, they also anticipated a fairly smooth transition.

Having worked in the neighborhood for years, Sophie knew that many of the buildings, including the one right next door to her new restaurant, were rumored to be haunted. Ghosts are considered to be part of the charm of the popular Whyte Avenue commercial strip, so that possible additional feature of the new business was never a concern.

In retrospect, the first oddity they noticed was that the men in the partnership seemed hesitant to get to the various chores that had to be done before the place could open. The men's reluctance was out of character and Sophie remembered thinking that "they seemed to have a strange sense of the place."

Despite this hesitancy, the work was about to begin when disaster struck. On March 13, 2003, with temperatures approaching -40°F, a fire broke out in the building next to the restaurant. Hours later, that structure was a heap of burned-out rubble and Sophie's new restaurant was completely inaccessible—sealed shut with ice from the water the firefighters had pumped out to control the blaze.

As soon as they were finally able to get inside, Sophie and her partners assessed the destruction and, amazingly, found that most of the damage was from flooding and very little was from the actual fire. The burned-out ruins of the building next door had to be bulldozed. At one point, the dozer operator accidentally drove through the wall into the restaurant, leaving a dangerously large hole. The wall amazingly held firm until it could be rebricked.

"Once the cleanup from the fire was through, the renovations started," Sophie recalled. The partners had no way of knowing that along with those renos would come tantalizing evidence of a most unusual haunting.

Sophie began by explaining, "The back hallway leading to the washrooms was a very dark space. It needed to be lightened up, so we chose a color with pink tones."

They had the paint mixed by a reputable dealer and, thinking that everything had been taken care of, Sophie's husband began painting the hallway. "He kept phoning us over at our other restaurant and asking us to come and check the color because it didn't seem to him that it was the shade that had been specified."

When she was able to join her husband at the new place, Sophie was shocked by what she saw. "The color was laughable! It was so vibrant. A neighboring merchant saw the shade and said it looked bubble-gum pink! It was not what we had wanted at all but, now that it was on the walls, we knew that we were not going to be able to make it disappear."

The partners decided that if they explained the problem to their supplier and had a special batch of paint mixed, they could apply that second color over the ridiculous one and perhaps come away with a reasonable shade.

"They had to redo and redo the solution. Eventually we ended up with the color that's on the walls now, a cranberry color. It was not what we wanted, but it would do," Sophie recalled.

Not long after that aggravation had been settled, the restaurant chairs arrived from a specialty manufacturer in another city. "We had wanted them in a brownish tone with no pink overtones. Five thousand dollars later, they're burgundy, a shade that definitely has pink overtones," Sophie related with understandable exasperation. "It was the same with the tables. The trim around the sides of the tabletops was supposed to match the chairs. It didn't."

The kitchen floor was the next issue they had to deal with. Like the paint color, the chairs and the tabletops, the floor came in the wrong shade. All of these mounting aggravations began to take a toll on the four people most closely involved with the project. Unfortunately, someone else was about to join their unenviable club.

Sophie explained, "We commissioned an artist to do a mural in the restaurant. We had seen lots of her work and really liked her style. She worked for us as a server at the other restaurant so we gave her time off to do the mural. We were surprised when she came to us one day and told us that she just couldn't do the painting. She was really upset and crying. She told us that she was giving up because no matter how hard she tried, it just wouldn't come out the way she wanted it to. We asked her to try again, which she did."

And, true to form with this new restaurant venture, the finished product is certainly attractive and very suitable—but the whimsical streetscape has a very different look than both the artist and owners expected.

Time after time, the four people involved in this enterprise were surprised at the constant aggravations they faced in getting the space ready for business. Just one little extra "bump" on the road to opening day gave them a clue as to what they were possibly dealing with.

Sophie's husband took on the job of scraping the accumulated layers of linoleum off the restaurant floor. As with all aspects of this renovation, the job proved to be much more of a chore than anyone had anticipated. When he was working on the floor, he kept hitting up against a lump. But it was a small bump and, considering all the work that had to be done, he was tempted just to leave it.

"He knew that I wouldn't be pleased, so he persisted," Sophie said.

And as he persisted, the reason for the bulge, and perhaps the reason for all the perplexing irritations, became visible. Hidden under several layers of old linoleum lay two gold rings—a man's and a woman's—tied together with a piece of cord.

No one knew what to make of this mysterious discovery.

Word of the poignant find soon spread throughout the quaint and close-knit commercial district. Many people thought that there must be an old love story connected to the two rings. When a local media outlet got wind of such an intriguing and potentially heartwarming human-interest story, they sent along a news team. The only problem was that uncovering the rings did nothing to stop the strange goings-on. Almost predictably, the television camera would not work once it was brought inside the restaurant. Outside, it worked just fine. Eventually the camera operator and the reporter were able to get their job done, but not without a great deal more effort than should have been necessary to cover this "fun" news story.

These rings apparently did not want their photo taken.

Not knowing what else to do with the rings, Sophie gave them to the building's owners. "But they didn't have any ideas about them and so they just gave them back to me."

Hoping that the news coverage about the find would draw the attention of someone who knew about the rings, Sophie left the two gold bands tied together as they were found and put them in a small container for safe keeping. Surely someone would come forward to answer the many questions that their discovery had posed.

For instance, were the rings' owners, like the rings, joined in some meaningful way? Who had the rings belonged to? Why weren't the rings still being worn, in life or in death? Were they ever worn, and if not, why not? When had they been hidden, and why was that particular spot under that particular floor chosen as a hiding place? Why had they been tied together? Who had tied them together?

To date no one has come forward with any answers.

As intriguing as the mystery was and is, Sophie and her partners still had to concentrate on running the restaurant. They decided that having a special blessing performed in such a business would be a good idea. Sophie's husband contacted a friend of his, a priest, and asked him to visit the restaurant and bless the place. Unfortunately, the priest didn't show up when he was supposed to. The man is a personal friend of the partners, and they were all very surprised that he didn't come. They knew him to be reliable. As it happens, the priest simply missed that first appointment, and the blessing was rescheduled.

Today, more than a year later, not much has changed in the cozy little restaurant or in the lives of its owners. "Light bulbs are always popping. For a while, the mantel sconce wouldn't stay lit, then it broke. We've let it remain broken. The windows were damaged when the exterior of the building was cleaned. The sign installer dropped the 'F' when he was installing the sign for the name of the restaurant. Instead of 'Flavours,' the shop was called 'lavours' for a weekend!" Sophie laughed, remembering those few days. "People were asking us if that was our name!"

Still smiling, the woman concluded, "The ghost is a trickster."

There's not much doubt about that in my mind. After interviewing Sophie, I tried to take a photograph of the rings. The camera I was using is one that I've had for five years. Up until that afternoon, it had never failed me. That day, despite my best attempts, my camera, like the television camera several months before, simply refused to work. I tried different locations and different light levels, but nothing I did would get the shutter to operate. Finally, laughing at the appropriateness of the situation, I turned to tell Sophie what was

Renovations to this café sometimes proceed at a ghostly pace.

happening. Just at that moment, the camera fired, resulting in a slightly blurred shot of questionable quality, but apparently that was the best I was going to get!

But what of the rings themselves? "I guess we'll get a little case for them and put them on display in the restaurant," Sophie told me. In the meantime, it's life as usual for the popular restaurant's owners. Even scheduling seems to present special difficulties in a building apparently haunted by love.

In an attempt to try to solve the mystery of the rings, experienced and efficient researcher Barrie W. Robinson, Ph.D., traced the occupancy of the Whyte Avenue address where the haunted Flavours is now located. The earliest reference to the building he was able to find was dated 1909, when the business operating from that address was a "pantorium" (clothes cleaner). Since then the place has housed a confectioner, a cigar manufacturer, a tailor, a shoemaker, a news agent, a grocery store and a jewelry store. The last might offer some explanation for the rings—but it still doesn't solve the mystery of this intriguing haunting.

First the Ring

Twenty years ago, a couple was traveling through British Columbia, Canada, on their way home to Calgary, Alberta. They stopped at a lake near Revelstoke. Having been cooped up in the car for a number of hours, they spent some time enjoying the fresh air and splashing about in the cool, refreshing water. By the time they were back on the road, both husband and wife felt refreshed and ready for the next leg of their journey. Not long after they began to head east again, the wife was upset to realize that her wedding ring was no longer on her finger.

"It must have slipped off my finger when I was wading in the lake," she told her husband, who offered to turn around and go back to the lake to look for the sentimental keepsake. After some discussion, they agreed the search would have about as much likelihood of success as finding the proverbial needle in a haystack.

Fifteen years later, while traveling that same stretch of highway leading to the lake, the couple's car suddenly veered off the road, perhaps to avoid wildlife or an oncoming car. No one knows for certain. All that is known is that both husband and wife drowned in the lake where she'd lost her wedding ring. Was it an eerie coincidence—or had the lost ring somehow been a precursor to the tragedy?

Lost and Found

The preceding enigmatic stories about wedding rings prompted my friend Nan to relate an incident that occurred in her family some 10 years ago. Kindly, she agreed to let me include this romantic and intriguing story in *Haunted Hearts*.

The story really began in 1914, when a young woman named Edith left her home in Owen Sound, Ontario, to join her married sister who was living on a farm near Belle Plaine, Saskatchewan. Not long after Edith arrived in the village on the Canadian Prairies, she met a man named Russell.

"He was a dashing red-haired young man from a neighboring farm," Nan related. "Eventually they became engaged."

Sadly, not long after the end of World War I, just as the young couple began to make plans to marry, Russell contracted liver disease and died. Needless to say, Russell's family as well as Edith, his fiancée, were devastated by the young man's death. Perhaps in part to help stave off the loneliness they both felt as a result of their loss, Edith and Jim, Russell's younger brother, began to spend time together.

"Soon Jim began escorting Edith to the dances and parties young people went to in those days," Nan said.

After the pair had dated casually in this manner for some time, it seems that "Jim finally gave Edith an ultimatum: marry me or move on."

What Jim's proposal lacked in romance it apparently made up for in effectiveness, because the couple who would eventually become Nan's grandparents were married in December 1923.

Like most young couples of that era, they did not have a lot of money. Edith's wedding ring was "just a simple gold band." Still, it was a treasured keepsake, and after Edith's death in the early 1980s, her daughter-in-law, Nan's mother, was honored to inherit that ring.

"My mother wore it after Grandma died. One year after Grandma died, Mom was cleaning up the garden for winter when she noticed the ring missing. Heartsick, she and my sister searched high and low for the ring, even dumping out the contents of the garbage bags they had filled with garden litter," Nan recalled.

Their search was fruitless. It seemed that Edith's wedding ring was lost forever.

Nan well remembered how distraught her mother had been. "Mom was very reluctant to tell Dad about the loss. I actually don't know if she ever did. She phoned me long distance and was nearly in tears as she told me about the lost ring."

Nan continued, "So, that winter passed into spring, then it was fall again, then spring. On Mother's Day, a full year and a half after the ring was lost, Mom was digging a trench for her annual display of sweet pea flowers beside the playhouse when she found the ring lying in the dirt."

After a momentary pause my friend added the final twist to the tale.

"Sweet peas were her own mother's favorite flower."

Lady in White

It was a cloudless night and the moon was nearly full. A young worker named John had been dispatched to do some repair work to the exterior of a lighthouse. The evening was calm and pleasant. It seemed almost impossible that this was the place where, only a month before, a deadly hurricane had tossed a ship against the rocky coastline, killing every soul on board except a tiny infant. Rescuers had found it clutched in the arms of its dead mother, whose remains had washed up onto the rocks below the lighthouse. The baby was soon adopted by a loving couple in town, and everyone, including John, tried to push the nightmare of the killer hurricane from their memories.

On this more recent night, John had nearly completed the assignment that had brought him to the lighthouse when an unexpected noise caught his attention. It sounded like the moan that the wind made as it blew around the shoreline. But it couldn't have been the wind because on this night the air was still.

John gave an involuntary shudder. Suddenly, inexplicably, he was chilled to the bone. He turned back to his work but, as he did, something caught his eye. He turned and stared in disbelief. There before him was the image of a woman—a woman wearing a ripped and tattered white dress. Her pathetic form floated toward John until it was so close that he could see her clearly—even the beseeching look in her eyes.

Terrified by what he had seen, John fled to the bunkhouse, where he found his coworkers relaxing.

"What's wrong, John?" one fellow asked when he saw the ashen-faced young man.

"I've just seen the strangest sight," John began.

Silence descended on the room as he related his experience. These were all men who worked closely with the sea and who heeded nautical superstitions and legends, many of which were ghost stories. To a man, they were sympathetic when they heard about John's otherworldly encounter. They were also afraid.

The next month and the month following that, the terrible image of the sad-looking woman in white was seen again. What haunted the witnesses most was the soul's obvious grief. How terrible, they all agreed, for her to have taken a broken heart into eternity.

News of the ghostly sightings soon spread to other communities, and before long it became impossible to keep staff at that lighthouse. No one wanted to risk running into the tormented and lonely ghost. A man named Jones, a lighthouse inspector at the time, is reported to have stated, "The apparition became known to all keepers in the service, many of whom were in deadly fear of the visitations. On one occasion, the head keeper was coming off watch at 10 PM and as he descended the spiral stairway of the tower, he observed the white phantom moving slowly up the stairs toward him. Her hooded head was bent forward. For some seconds he remained rooted to the spot, paralyzed with fright. Steadily the figure advanced toward him. Just as he was recovering his senses sufficiently to turn and run, the figure stopped and then vanished."

Others also had the misfortune to see the apparition. Some, like John, maintained that they had heard the ghost's heart-wrenching moans. A few witnesses were haunted by the dreadful look in the phantom's eyes as she raised her head and looked pleadingly into their eyes, evidently looking for help—help that no mortal could give.

Many years later, the man who had freed the baby from its dead mother's arms received word of the haunting. His experience on that long-ago night during the hurricane reinforced the trauma of the event, perhaps offering some explanation for the existence of the tragic, earthbound soul. He explained that he would never forget the horror of having to pry the tiny baby from the corpse of the child's mother and then having to carry the infant to the home of the couple who eventually adopted the little one.

In an attempt to lay the tortured entity to rest, the baby's rescuer and some other people associated with the lighthouse chose a spot as close as possible to where the woman's earthly remains had been found. There, they held a service to commemorate her passing.

For many years that makeshift exorcism was thought to have been successful—and perhaps to a degree it was, for since that time there have been only a few appearances of the heartsick ghost. One of those sightings was near the home where her orphaned baby had been taken years before.

Interestingly, this heartbroken apparition in her tattered white dress is seen only on nights of a nearly full moon.

Ghost Finds Peace

In south-central England, nestled in the beautiful Kennet Valley, lies the village of Ramsbury. Some 75 years ago, that village was home to a very haunted house.

Samuel and Mary Jane Bull had lived contented lives in their tiny Ramsbury cottage for many years before Samuel passed away. Although she missed him terribly, Mary Jane coped well enough on her own until eventually she, too, became ill. The couple's married daughter saw that her mother was suffering and so decided to move back home to care for her. The younger woman's intentions were no doubt kind enough, but in reality the plan didn't work very well because she had a family of her own and therefore brought her husband and five children with her. The Bulls' small house became intolerably crowded.

Little did the people living in those cramped quarters know that the place was about to get even more crowded!

One of the children was the first to see the manifestation of Mary Jane's deceased husband. The child recognized the image as he climbed the stairs, apparently to tend to his grandmother's needs. Only the ghost's widow was not distressed about the sighting, because over the months since his death Mary Jane had come to enjoy her deceased husband's loving visits. He often sat with her when she wasn't feeling well and even brushed her brow with his ghostly hand as if to soothe her.

After a time, the family was able to move to a larger house and from that day on Samuel Bull's spirit was never seen again. Perhaps he was able to rest peacefully knowing that his loved ones, his wife in particular, were now living in more comfortable quarters.

Home Is Where the Heart Is

Cape Breton, Nova Scotia, is a land of coal miners—and ghosts.

In the Canadian Maritimes, supernatural activity tends to be readily accepted. Perhaps the dangers of both the sea and underground coal mining have somehow helped to promote such acceptance. The following story is a good example of both the dangers of mining and of Maritime ghostly activity.

On a warm, summer afternoon, many, many years ago, two women were chatting near their homes. Suddenly, one of the women saw her husband, John, coming home from work and walking into their house. She broke off her conversation immediately and excused herself from her friend to check on her husband who, she presumed, must have taken ill. Otherwise he would never have left the mine before his shift was over.

As the woman's neighbor turned to return to her home, she saw her own husband walking toward her. "Hello," he called. "Sad news, I'm afraid. John was killed in an accident at the mine not half an hour ago."

Ghostly Fall from Grace

Grace Brown was probably as relieved as she was pleased when Chester Gillette invited her to go away for a few days with him. She was sure that he was finally going to do the right thing by her—and it was about time. When they had started "keeping company" a few months before, Chester had insisted that their relationship should remain a secret. Grace initially understood his hesitancy. A policy at the Cortland, New York, skirt factory where they both worked clearly stated that the men in the company were forbidden from fraternizing with the women employees. As the weeks went by and they continued to see each other, Grace became somewhat less accepting of the supposed need for secrecy.

Had Grace not been so naive, she might have been suspicious of Chester's motives right from the beginning. After all, Chester's uncle owned the skirt factory and it was generally known that Chester was being groomed for an important position in the company. A relationship with a common seamstress from the factory floor would not do much to enhance his future. When Grace discovered she was pregnant, she confronted Chester and tried to insist that he marry her.

Sadly, from Chester's point of view, there was nothing simple about doing the "right thing," for he was not leading a simple life. As a matter of fact, Chester Gillette was leading a double life. His other girlfriend not only stood several rungs above Grace on the social ladder but also had the added appeal of not being pregnant.

After trying unsuccessfully to avoid Grace, the young man suggested that the two of them get away together for a few days. Chester's idea of a trip to South Bay on nearby Big Moose Lake sounded exactly like the escape Grace so badly needed, especially as she hoped the journey would include a visit to a justice of the peace. Chester, too, wanted the trip to solve the problem of Grace and her pregnancy, but his solution did not include marriage.

And so, with very different agendas, the young couple headed to the lake. When Chester first suggested renting a rowboat, Grace was hesitant because she had never learned to swim. Using the charm that had won him the young woman's affections in the first place, Chester soon convinced Grace that there was nothing in the world quite as relaxing as a leisurely ride in a boat on a nice calm lake. Less than an hour later, Chester swam to shore, leaving the rowboat to sink. Grace and the unborn child were already at the bottom of the lake.

The most poignant part of the tragedy is that Gillette might even have been able to get away with murder if he hadn't rented the boat in the first place. The owner of the small craft wondered what had happened to his property, and contacted the police to report that his rowboat had been stolen.

Grace's body was found the following day. By the time the week was up, Chester Gillette had been arrested and charged with murder. His trial captured worldwide attention and lasted for nearly two years. Although it was based solely on circumstantial evidence, at the end of the proceedings Gillette was found guilty and executed.

Even though the "lovers" were no longer alive, the world could not forget them. For years after Chester Gillette's deadly deed, there was talk about the couple, the crime and the trial, which had presumably at least wrought justice from the horrors. Books, a movie and a play have all been written about the July 1906 murder in New York State's beautiful Adirondack Mountains.

As recently as the late 1980s, sightings of the ghost of a young woman have been reported near the place where she drowned some 80 years before. The paranormal encounter seemed to sensitize witnesses to Grace's presence, because after that they reported additional strange, seemingly other-worldly events in the area.

Those reports were taken seriously enough for the long-running television show *Unsolved Mysteries* to feature a segment on the haunting and its gruesome background. The show's producers recreated some of the supernatural events, such as a wispy ribbon of smoke seen hovering near where people were walking. A flashlight inexplicably gets dimmer in the area where the ghost was seen and then returns to full power once the person holding it walks a bit farther along. One witness spoke of a feeling of great discomfort and sadness, while another forthrightly explained that she had seen what she knew to be the ghost of Grace Brown. She recognized the woman's features from a picture she had seen.

By now, a century has passed since the unfortunate young woman was drowned in Big Moose Lake. Perhaps Grace's spirit has found the eternal peace that eluded her for so long.

The Perfect Love Story

Climatologists call the collision of three particular types of weather systems "the perfect storm." But weather is a physical phenomenon. Surely it would be a fool's game to try to identify the ingredients necessary for "the perfect love story." But where love is concerned, we're probably all fools sometimes, so let's try.

For starters, the equation would have to include the lovers themselves. Preferably both would be talented and attractive folk devoted to a worthy occupation that makes a positive contribution to the world. If the path to true love ran smoothly, then the love story wouldn't have much of a plotline, so we must add a villain to the mix, a villain powerful enough to jeopardize the lovers' dreams. After a monumental struggle against the villain, the pair must be able to overcome all obstacles and live happily—but only for a time. If the old adage holds that "the course of true love never runs smoothly," then there are bound to be more challenges or obstacles to their mutual devotion.

This, then, is perhaps a recipe for the romantic

Robert Schumann

equivalent of "the perfect storm." Now, add a paranormal event—or even several paranormal events—and you would have a remarkable tale of Haunted Hearts.

Clara Wieck was only nine years old when composer Robert Schumann first laid eyes on her. Despite her age, the girl was already an accomplished pianist whose talents Schumann openly admired. It is probably safe to assume that Clara's father, Friedrich Wieck, would have been pleased by the composer's admiration of the girl's abilities because it was Wieck's intention that his daughter would become a concert pianist.

But, eight years later in 1836, when Schumann asked for Clara's hand in marriage, Friedrich Wieck was not nearly so pleased. As a matter of fact, he was outraged. Schumann's request was promptly and soundly denied. Clara's future was to be a pianist on the stages of Europe's greatest concert halls, not to be the wife of a composer. Wieck forbade the two from seeing one another.

For four long years, the determined father attempted to prevent Schumann from communicating with Clara as she toured, performing to appreciative audiences. Despite the older man's best efforts, though, the two were occasionally able to exchange letters. In one of Schumann's missives to his beloved Clara he urged her, "Love me; love me well. I ask for much because I give much."

Throughout these years when the two were forced to be apart, Schumann composed loving musical tributes to Clara—and some historians maintain that he also wrote music inspired by his love for other women.

When Clara returned home from her tours, she and Schumann were again at least in the same city (Leipzig, Germany). Their proximity made Friedrich Wieck's mandate virtually impossible for them to obey and, on September 12, 1839, the day before Clara's 21st birthday, the long-thwarted pair secretly wed.

The marriage was a happy one. The couple toured together performing, studying and composing. In due course, they became the proud parents of four children.

But this story is not a fairy tale and the couple was not to live happily ever after, for Schumann's lifelong inclination to "melancholia" had returned. This time, the depression was made worse by the addition of an auditory hallucination—the constant sound of the note "A" ringing in his ears.

As the weeks and months went by, the composer's hallucinations became worse. Eventually, he heard what he described as "great symphonic pieces played right through." Later, he spoke of hearing the voices of angels and of writing down the notes they sang.

Clara became frantic. When Schumann told Clara that the ghosts of Franz Schubert and Felix Mendelssohn, whose compositions he greatly admired, had come to him in a dream and given him a beautiful musical theme, she refused to allow the piece to be published. She was afraid that her formerly well-respected husband's interaction with the spirit world would cause him to be ridiculed.

When the supernatural forces impinging on Schumann's mind changed from angelic and benign to demonic, the composer became terrified. He was afraid that he would do something to hurt either Clara or one of their children. And so, on February 27, 1854, Robert Schumann quietly left the family home and hurried to a bridge over the Rhine River. There, in an attempt to end his misery once and for all, he threw himself into the waters below. As fate would have it, a passerby witnessed the attempted suicide and reached the drowning man in time to save his life. From that day until he died on July 29, 1856, Schumann was a patient at a private asylum.

And whatever became of the music given to Schumann by the ghosts of the long-dead composers? Johannes Brahms, who some people maintain was a devoted family friend but others say was madly in love with Clara, reworked the pieces after Schumann's death. Even today, the "Ghost Variations," as the pieces have come to be called, are frequently performed and enjoyed all over the world.

Lovers' Lane

Almost every town has one: a lovers' lane. In this secluded spot, people with romance on their minds can find that bit of privacy their hearts so desire.

Ghost stories are often connected to such spots. Perhaps the legends that haunt these isolated areas are just foolishness. Perhaps it is only the excitement lovers feel at being alone, hidden away together with all of their senses heightened, that teases the human imagination into thinking something extraordinary—even supernatural—is at work in these secret locales.

Of course it's equally possible that the ghost stories are true—as true as the documented tale of a haunting near Hempstead, Long Island.

There is a small inlet at a certain point on a river near Hempstead. At that tiny bay, a smaller watercourse meanders into the river. For years locals have called the stream Lovers' Creek. In the early 1800s, the area surrounding this tranquil setting was remote and isolated, and it became a popular place for young couples seeking some treasured private moments.

One such couple was deeply in love and met at the creek as often as they could. On the day of their last meeting, the young maiden was feeling ill. Nevertheless, she made her way to their rendezvous. As soon as he saw her walking toward him, the young man knew that something was desperately wrong. The girl he loved, who was usually full of energy and the absolute picture of health, moved painfully slowly. Worse, she looked pale and drawn. As he reached to embrace her, the girl collapsed in a lifeless heap at his feet. The young man tried desperately to revive her, but it was too late—the girl he loved had died.

Devastated by his loss and perhaps frightened that he would be accused of murdering her, the man drew his pistol and killed himself with a single shot to the head. His body fell next to hers, and there the two were found some time later.

To honor the couple and their terrible tragedy, the inconsequential waterway became known as Lovers' Creek. It also became quite famous—locally at least—as a haunted place. People who dared visit the spot often reported sensing a subtle shift in the atmosphere around them. Some witnesses described this telltale change as an aroma. Others spoke of the air around them as seeming to crackle with energy, while still others simply reported feeling lightheaded. No matter how the living perceived the initial paranormal intrusion, what followed was always the same—the sudden sight of a young man and a young woman, hand in hand, strolling beside the creek.

According to newspaper reports, the lovers were "living out, in ghostly form, the existence whose earthly career was interrupted in such a melancholy manner."

But how is it that those who have seen the couple are sure they are being offered a glimpse into the supernatural? Well, you see, the pair strolling by the creek don't *walk* so much as *glide* along, just above the ground. The other clue that neither the young man nor the young woman belongs on this earth is that their bodies are ever-so-slightly see-through.

More recently, people have even seen the ghostly lovers sitting happily in a spectral boat as it floats along the stream's gentle current. And so, at least at Lovers' Creek on Long Island, New York, the stories of entities loving long into the afterlife are absolutely true—as true as the tragedy of their young love.

Another Lovers' Lane

The following story, which also involves a haunted lovers' lane, is such a sad tale that even without the ghost's presence, it is poignant enough to haunt a heart.

In 1912, Sylvia Scott was born at her parents' home in the pretty countryside southwest of Richmond, Indiana. Sylvia's mother treasured her second daughter, but some people who knew the family suspected that neither Mr. Scott nor Betty, the couple's older daughter, loved the child quite so much. When Sylvia was still in her teens, her mother was committed to a mental health hospital, leaving the girl to fend for herself against her cold and domineering father and sister.

The two kept Sylvia at home and, it was thought, treated her more like a servant than a family member. Any young man who ever showed an interest in the girl was soon shooed away. Before long, the happy young lady who loved to sing became a depressed and withdrawn adult. By the time she was 31, Sylvia had followed in her mother's footsteps by being committed to an institution, where she died just five years later. Her father and older sister arranged to have the body cremated and the ashes scattered over the hillside near their home.

And that was the end of Sylvia Scott's unhappy life.

Her afterlife, it seemed, had just begun. One winter's night in 1965, Dale Vaughn and his high school sweetheart, Joan Groce, drove to a deserted country road southwest of Richmond. Dale chose a spot that appeared to be private and parked the car. As far as either Joan or Dale could see, there were no other cars in the area. Nevertheless, before long they were both sure that they had heard the sound of car doors slamming closed. Startled and puzzled, Dale grabbed his flashlight and went to investigate the intruders that they could not see. After shining the light around and seeing nothing unexpected, he started back to the car.

Then, a movement in the distance caught his eye. He shone the flashlight in that direction and, for an instant, he could see an image he was sure was that of a girl walking. Seconds later, impossibly, the image vanished from sight. He hurried back to Joan's side, and the couple joked that Dale must have been seeing things. Moments later, however, their laughter stopped. There, behind the car, was the readily identifiable figure of a female. The apparition was so clear that they saw its long dark hair, a blouse so white that it seemed to glow and a distinctive checked skirt. Dale and Joan might even have believed that they had seen a flesh-and-blood person—except that the apparition had no face, and rather than walking it seemed to glide perfectly smoothly just above the road. Then, as they watched in horror, the manifestation became less and less solid before disappearing completely.

Dale, easily as terrified by what they'd seen as Joan was, started the car, turned it around and drove quickly away.

In the spring of that year, another young couple, Leroy Forrest and Mary McKay, drove to the lovers' lane. They too were frightened away by the sight of a form floating near their car.

It is not known whether either of those two couples ever again sought out the privacy of that particular country road, but Dale's brother Howard, who was dating Joan's sister Jaynie, ventured to the spot one autumn evening later in that same year. They hadn't been stopped long when something moving behind the car caught Jaynie's attention. Howard didn't even look around when his girlfriend screamed that the ghost was beside the car. He'd heard the stories and had no desire to have an encounter with the faceless phantom. Howard turned the key in the ignition, threw the car into gear and sped away from the haunted area. Once they reached safety, Jaynie described the specter she had seen—the body of a female with long dark hair but no visible arms, legs or face, wearing a radiant white blouse.

On a spring day in 1966, two teenage boys were hiking in the area when they looked down the hillside and saw a "foggy, white image" hovering over the ground. When they realized that what they'd seen was not of this world, they ran back in the direction from which they'd come.

About this time, the occupants of a house near that country road began to hear phantom sounds around their home. These sounds persisted for years, and once, in the summer of 1969, one member of the household watched in fascination as a luminous white figure floated about their yard before disappearing.

By this time, word of the strange sightings had spread throughout the neighboring communities. Writer-investigator Don Worley, along with his nephew Jack, decided to investigate. They had only just arrived near the place where the sightings had been reported when they felt "a concussive sensation" in their ears "similar to that produced by the slamming of a car door." Moments later, a bright, white being appeared near them and quickly floated along before disappearing from sight.

Fascinated by the implications of what they had seen, the pair began to ask questions of the people who lived near the area. It wasn't long before they heard the heartbreakingly sad story of Sylvia Scott's short, unhappy life. They were also told that in her teenage years she had favored white blouses and often wore a distinctive checked skirt. She had also worn her dark hair long.

Sylvia's spirit, it seemed, was determined to have the carefree afterlife that the circumstances of her earthly life did not allow her to enjoy.

Riding Wraith

The year was 1903 and a ghost story was making international news. Headlines from the Saint John, New Brunswick, *Daily Sun* on July 4 read:

A SPECTRE ON HORSE BACK
Comes Back to Pennsylvania City to Terrify People
Wraith Again Riding a Horse–
Weird Story of Revolutionary Days
Recalled When Reprieve Failed to Save Girl

On July 1, 1903, in the haunted city of Chester, Pennsylvania, crowds of hopeful ghost-watchers lined the streets, much as expectant crowds had lined those same streets some 118 years before. On both occasions the citizens of the quiet community south of Philadelphia were hoping to catch a glimpse of a particular man on horseback—William Wilson. Of course in 1785, it was the living William Wilson that the people were hoping to see riding toward them. In 1903, it was his ghost astride an equally ghostly steed.

When the events of this story began to unfold way back in the 18th century, young William Wilson was working the fields of a farm in Lancaster County, Pennsylvania. His work was mindless and yet satisfying. The sun warmed his strong back and the soft breeze cooled it. His thoughts wandered aimlessly as one's thoughts do at such times. Suddenly an image of his sister Elizabeth came strongly to his mind. At first the man smiled; he'd always been fond of his sister. As children growing up in East Bradford, he and Elizabeth had been exceptionally close. His thoughts of her now, though, were quickly becoming uncomfortable—crowding out all other thoughts.

William began to feel panicky. *Strange that Elizabeth would come to my mind with such force at this moment. We haven't seen each other for nearly two years.* Elizabeth was staying with relatives, and surely, he thought, they would help her if she were in trouble in any way. Breathing a stuttered sigh and shaking his head, William tried to chase the worry from his mind. But the fear he felt convinced him that his beloved sister was in some danger. He had to see her. He ran from the field toward the barn where his horse was tethered. As fast as he could, William Wilson set out to ride to Chester.

Twice during his frenzied ride, Wilson wondered if he was acting impulsively, possibly foolishly. After all, he'd had no word that Elizabeth was in distress—well, none except the overwhelming psychic message he was responding to.

It wasn't until the exhausted horse and rider reached Chester that Wilson learned that Elizabeth was indeed in grave danger. The unshakable thoughts of his sister had been an urgent telepathic plea.

While living at their relatives' boarding house, the pretty young woman had fallen in love with an ex-colonel in the army who, according to the 1903 article in the *Daily Sun*, "paid her marked attention." People had tried to tell Elizabeth that the man was a cad, but she wouldn't listen. As time would prove, the former officer was not a cad at all—calling such an evil dastard a "cad" would have been a compliment, for he soon deserted Miss Wilson and the infant twin boys their relationship had produced.

Elizabeth was frantic with worry. How could she hold her head up in society? Not only was she unmarried, but now there was no hope she ever would be. And what of the sheer practical matters? How could she support herself and her two dear sons?

This tragic tale was about to take a turn for the worse. To quote the *Daily Sun's* report: "Ten months later the bodies of the infants were found in the woods...Elizabeth Wilson was tried for murder in Chester's old court house and convicted. The court fixed Wednesday, December 7, 1785 as the day of execution."

It was at the very moment of her sentencing that the young woman's brother had telepathically sensed his sister's terrible distress and had set out to be at her side—in a jail cell, awaiting death by hanging. Despite intense questioning, Elizabeth had remained mute during her trial. It wasn't until she saw William that the brokenhearted and wrongly convicted girl divulged the truth about the monstrous crime. "The father of the children was the murderer," she told her brother.

Armed with the truth, William Wilson then immediately rode to Philadelphia, where he hoped to have his sister's death sentence reprieved. Day after day, he waited for a chance to speak to someone with the power to stay the execution. Finally, on the rain-soaked morning of Elizabeth's scheduled execution, a man identified only as "Dr. Franklin" granted the request. The young woman's name had been cleared, her life saved—if William could reach the gallows in Chester before the hangman performed his heinous deed.

Despite William's skill and determination, and the terrible urgency of the life-and-death circumstances, his ride back was a painfully slow one. "Heavy rains had greatly swollen the streams and the ferry was not being operated over the Schuylkill," the newspaper report detailed, "but horse and rider plunged in and, after a heroic struggle, reached the other shore. All the creeks had to be forded and Wilson's progress was everywhere retarded."

Elizabeth had given up all hope of ever seeing another sunrise. Even the crowds of people lining the streets leading out of Chester did nothing to buoy her spirits, although she knew each one was there watching for her brother's return with a reprieve. By this time, even the authorities were hoping the young man would reach town in time to save Elizabeth Wilson's life. "The sheriff delayed his grim duties until the last minute," but inevitably that fated minute did come and "the wagon that formed the scaffold was pulled from beneath the unhappy woman."

With tragic irony, at that very instant, "a signal came from a far-off watcher and a few minutes later, William Wilson, on a mud-stained horse, rode up waving a paper frantically and calling, 'Reprieve!'

"Then with a heart-rending cry as his eyes caught sight of the limp form dangling from the rope, he fell in a swoon, from which he was aroused an hour later—grey-haired—an old man in a day. Years afterward, a long-bearded hermit died in his cabin on a mountain in Dauphin County. He was William Wilson."

For years the community was haunted by the dreadful miscarriage of justice. According to the newspaper report 118 years later, "upon the anniversary of the trial the superstitious saw a spectral rider gallop at midnight on the same fruitless journey." People watched in horror as the ghostly image disappeared from sight when it reached the spot where the old jailhouse had stood.

As dramatic and lovelorn as that old ghost story might be, it is still amazing that the tale was not forgotten. After all, the terrible events that caused the haunting took place in 1785! The same newspaper article acknowledges, "The story and the rider would have remained forgotten or unknown by the great majority of Chester people had not the spectre resumed his ghostly dash along the street upon which once stood the old jail in which Elizabeth Wilson was a prisoner."

More disturbing still was that a sighting of the apparition soon became recognized as an omen "for some deed of blood in that neighborhood. Two Philadelphia murderers were found taking refuge there; a dozen shooting and stabbing affrays have occurred on the street and Albert West came from a house in that quarter a few minutes before he shot and killed Officer Mark W. Allen." For those reasons even the police began to take notice whenever the ghost of William Wilson was seen.

This haunting story is made even more interesting, and perhaps additionally troubling, because Elizabeth has never returned to join the ghost of her brother who loved her so deeply. Perhaps she simply acknowledges in invisible silence and resignation that her brother's ghostly gallop will, once again, be in vain.

Past Death Do Us Part

This next story plays with your imagination. It is based on an incident that occurred somewhere in the Qu'Appelle Valley of Saskatchewan, Canada. I have simply imagined the spirit of the murdered wife, a woman removed from a marriage to make room for another woman. It is, if you will, a ghost-written ghost story.

"For richer and for poorer, in sickness and in health, till death us do part" were the vows I'd taken 28 years ago. And they were vows I'd kept—until this morning. This morning I was released from my obligations. Somehow it seemed strangely ironic that my emancipator had actually been Julia, a woman I had never even considered in the role of savior. She was an enemy, an enemy of longstanding, from the very beginning—from that summer day in 1894 when she first laid eyes on my husband, Matthew.

The love between the two of them had been obvious right from the start. I fought for years to retain both my dignity and my marriage, but after a while it became clearly and painfully evident that Matthew and I were married in name only. He loved Julia, but didn't have the courage to leave me and the security I represented, security that she, most assuredly, did not. From then on, I could do nothing but hold my head up and pretend it wasn't happening. What else could I have done?

Oh, I tried to remind him that he had prospered only with my support and that not all women would have been able, or willing, to take on as much as I had. It had always been I who had been sure to set aside a little something at the end of each year. And my determination had paid off. After almost 30 years we had accumulated a tidy sum—actually, a very tidy sum—a sum ten times greater than he even knew about. But none of that mattered anymore. Now, all I needed to do was stand back and watch unfold the unfortunate circumstances that Matthew and Julia had created.

It had been so quick—quick and surprisingly painless. I was dead before I knew it. They'd planned it well, that much was certain. Julia approached the front door with a hard, determined look about her. I'd thought she was coming to confront me, but she had been just a decoy. Seconds after I saw her walk up the path to the house, everything went black. Using her supposed visit as a distraction, Matthew had placed himself directly behind me, his gun at the base of my skull—pointing just slightly upward.

Once the blackness faded, I seemed to be able to float back and forth, in and out of my body. I watched them working, almost in unison and at a fevered pace. It was clear from their determined moves that they had rehearsed this, at least in their minds, many times.

Covered in my blood from his head to his shoes, Matthew reached toward the grandfather clock that had stood in our living room since the day we were married. At the same time as he was pulling it down, he turned it around. The back of the enormous timepiece hit the floor with a thud. Julia unlocked the pendulum case and threw open its glass door. She looked over at Matthew and, when she saw he was at the head of my bloodied body, she moved to my ankles. Together, they fought to cram my lifeless body inside the clock. Then, one at each end, they labored to carry their load outside to the wagon. I could feel my former self being bumped along the rough trail and wondered, vaguely, where they were headed with their incriminating load.

A clock as my coffin, I thought with an unexpected laugh. *How timely.*

Suddenly I wondered—if I could hear them, which I could, then could they also hear me? If so, I'd better not be lying in here, deader than yesterday's catch, giggling at my own silly puns.

With each bump in the path I became more and more convinced that we were heading to the lake. They intended to throw the clock, with my body as an anchor, into the deep, black waves of the lake that for so many years had provided us with life-sustaining food and water.

I nearly laughed again when I realized my nest egg—well, "our" nest egg—a collection of rare, slim, handwritten, centuries-old books, would be ruined, rendered worthless the moment the water surged around them. At the time that I'd purchased these precious volumes, I'd prided myself on my ingenuity. Matthew didn't know about my investment. Even if he had found them, he couldn't have spent that portion of our savings impulsively. Not only were the bills of sale in my name, but resale would have to be arranged through an auction house. Matthew wouldn't have known the first thing about how such a process worked.

None of that mattered now anyway. I was dead. The lovers had what they thought they wanted—each other. My collection of fine books lay behind the panel of wood that Matthew had always thought was simply the back of the clock.

His grunts of exertion were accompanied by the sounds of wood scraping against wood as they worked my clock-coffin from the wagon onto the deck of our small boat.

"Just keep your grip a moment longer," I could hear Matthew order in a strained voice, but his admonition came too late. The clock dropped to the deck. Inside, my lifeless body jostled about and then rearranged itself against the false back where the valuable books were hidden.

Waves slapped and thumped at the bottom of the boat. We were apparently heading out from shore. Then the forward motion stopped. Moments later, he and Julia struggled to dump the clock into the water. Slowly at first, and then with a little more speed, my entombed body sank until it jolted to a stop on the silty lake bottom. After a few seconds of shifting and settling, all was still.

Again, I wanted to laugh—this time wryly. I doubted that either Matthew or Julia could hear me now, but even so, I was relieved when I managed to regain my self-control. I knew they'd be rowing back to shore by now. I also knew that the pages of my ancient, handwritten investments were now smeared, soggy and worthless.

I bided my time. Time was something I had a great deal of now. I was at rest, in complete darkness and silence. Why, from here, I could even have gone directly to my final reward. *But,* I thought, *I have a little unfinished business to attend to first.*

I reached underneath me and pried up a corner of the false backing that had hidden my investments so well for so many years. Barely able to reach even one book at first, I realized that it didn't matter one whit if I didn't happen to get a firm hold on an entire volume. All I needed was to be able to grasp a cover and a few pages.

Once I had half a dozen pieces of paper and a portion of a book's cover clutched in my hands, I waited until I guessed it was close to midnight. Then, careful not to lose my grasp on the pages, I let myself float to the surface of the lake before making my way to the shore near my house. Well, the house that had been mine.

I went quietly through the front door. Matthew and Julia were asleep in the bed that Matthew and I had shared for nearly three decades. Both were snoring heavily. If their consciences were troubling them, the exhaustion from their labors had overridden any possible guilt-provoked insomnia. I didn't disturb the sleeping couple, just walked to the kitchen, laid the still-wet book cover and a few ink-stained leaves of parchment on the kitchen table. The gold-engraved lettering on the cover's spine would provide a clue as to what the soggy, illegible pages once contained. Satisfied, I left again by the front door.

As I turned back to take one last look into the home that had been mine for all of my marriage, I noticed that I'd left a trail of wet, muddy footprints across the floor from the front door to the bedroom, into the kitchen, and then back to the door. I smiled a satisfied smile as I pondered my murderers' reactions when they saw the unearthly mess I'd created in "their" house. I even entertained the thought of staying behind to see them for myself. But, really, there was no need.

The score had been evened. I was ready to meet my maker.

Dying to Marry

One by one, the wedding guests, whose gaiety had filled and brightened the huge hall, fell completely silent. Then scattered gasps broke the silence, followed by several heavy thumps—the kind of terrible thump that a human body makes when it falls to the floor in a dead faint. Suddenly, an icy chill swept through the enormous room as heavy, lurching, metallic-sounding footfalls clanked their way across the stone floor.

"Who are you?" the host of the party demanded.

"Ask her!" the armor-clad figure growled, pointing a bloody, skeletal finger at the bride. "Aye, she had my body killed, but, as you can see, my spirit has survived—at least long enough for me to curse you and her and the traitor who did this to me. Mark my words, King Alexander III of Scotland, your happy reign is nearly over. Within six months you will be dead. Your subjects will turn against your new queen and she will die in poverty after great suffering. For years and years, peace will be unknown in your kingdom."

With those words, the hideous armored figure vanished, leaving only its blood-stained ghostly footprints on the castle floor and, of course, the legacy of its dreadful curse on the land and all of its inhabitants.

King Alexander III of Scotland had been a lad of seven when he ascended to the throne in 1249. As ridiculous as that might seem to us today, a boy king was actually a fairly common occurrence at that time. What wasn't common was an unmarried king, and so, at the age of 10, the monarch married Princess Margaret from England's royal family. The marriage lasted until February 1275, when Margaret died, leaving three children as potential heirs for her husband.

Sadly, not one of the three lived for more than 10 years after their mother's death.

The widowed and now childless Alexander decided that he must find a new wife and produce another heir to his throne. Alexander began making arrangements for a huge party to be held at his home, Scotland's Jedburgh Castle.

As the day of the gala event dawned, guests (especially marriageable women) from all over the British Isles made their way to the south of Scotland. All but one of those hopeful lasses might just as well have stayed home, because after King Alexander III set his eyes upon Yolande, the gorgeous daughter of France's ambassador, his majesty's heart had been won.

For her part, Yolande was so flattered to have been chosen over all the beautiful young women at the party that she would have done anything to keep the king's affections. And she did—she forgot that she had already been promised in marriage to a knight in her father's court. Before the absent-minded young woman had time to begin concerning herself with this little problem, another of her father's knights, a man named de Montbar, approached her and whispered evil and tempting words in her ear.

"Your father is a man of honor. He will never agree to let you marry the Scottish king while the knight you are engaged to is still alive. If you promise me a place at your side in the kingdom you will share with Alexander, I will arrange to have your fiancé's life ended."

Despite the horrible implications of the man's offer, Yolande knew he was right. Her father would never let her marry Alexander after promising her hand in marriage to one of his bravest knights. Without saying a word, the ambitious Yolande nodded in agreement with the evil man's monstrous plan.

No further messages were exchanged between de Montbar and Yolande, but a few days later the knight who was to have wed the French ambassador's daughter was found stabbed to death in a nearby forest. An investigation into the murder began immediately, but was soon set aside in the wake of the exciting announcement of the upcoming royal wedding. King Alexander III and his beloved Yolande were to be married in the abbey adjoining Jedburgh Castle in the autumn of 1285.

On the day of the wedding, the jilted man's body, clad in armor, lay cold in its grave. His soul, however, was anxious for revenge and that was exactly what possessed his spirit as it trudged the remains of its earthly self into the banquet hall and uttered its unearthly curses.

King Alexander died less than six months later after a freak fall from the back of a horse. His subjects blamed his wily new wife for their king's death. Some revolted against her, creating upheaval that would eventually become a long and bloody civil war. And, as predicted, Yolande died in poverty, having left a terrible legacy of her time on earth. To the end, the conniving de Montbar kept his word and never left her side. His company, however, was part of Yolande's burden, for he had suffered a paralyzing stroke and become an invalid not long after the royal wedding he had helped orchestrate. The ghostly curse had come to pass.

Endless Love

For years, every August 23, just as morning gave way to afternoon, the click-clack staccato of high-heel pumps on a stone floor echoed through the hallways of Hollywood Forever's Cathedral Mausoleum. No one ever knew much about the stately woman who wore those shoes except that she was dressed all in black from her fashionable footwear to her formal black hat, and that once a year she carried a bouquet of flowers to a particular crypt. After placing the floral arrangement and pausing to pay her respects, the shadow-like being turned and slowly walked back into the shroud of mystery that cloaked her identity as surely as the heavy black veil she always wore over her face.

By now, no one can ever know for certain the identity of this enigmatic and devoted being. Why she made the annual pilgrimage, however, is no secret. Like tens of thousands of other women alive during the mid-1920s, she had obviously fallen under the spell of Hollywood's "Great Lover," Rudolph Valentino.

Valentino rose to a level of stardom that is difficult for today's moviegoers to understand. Moving pictures were a new and fascinating

Rudolf Valentino

phenomenon when the lithe, handsome young man from Italy made his debut on the silver screen. His dark, even features, his slim body so exquisitely trained in the art of dance, were the answer to every woman's private fantasies and to every studio boss's fondest dreams. Even though his first roles were only bit parts, the strikingly handsome man's persona came through so well on camera that Valentino stole any show he was in and also the heart of every woman in the audience.

Over the course of only seven years, Rudolph Valentino made 14 movies and became an absolute sensation. Women loved him; men emulated him.

Then tragedy struck. On August 23, 1926, the collective hearts of movie fans all over the world broke. The dynamic life of the silver screen's Great Lover, begun only 31 years before, had ended in a New York City hospital. Valentino had died after undergoing emergency surgery to repair severe abdominal problems. The furor over Valentino's passionate and romantic soul, however, had just begun.

As word of his death spread from the hospital corridors to the sidewalks of New York City, women streamed out into the streets. Mass hysteria ensued. At least two women and one man killed themselves after hearing the news of the actor's death. By the time Valentino's funeral service drew to a close a week later, an estimated 100,000 mourners had viewed the idol's body as it lay in state almost hidden by tens of thousands of floral tributes.

Valentino's pallbearers were a veritable who's who of the fledgling movie world. Immediately after the funeral service in New York, the Great Lover's body was shipped to Hollywood, where it would be laid to rest.

Death had apparently been the furthest thing from the 31-year-old movie star's mind, and he had not made any provisions for his own cemetery plot. As a result, he was temporarily entombed in a crypt owned by June Mathis, a woman who had been instrumental in introducing the Great Lover and the film industry to one another. When Mathis herself died just a few months later, appropriate arrangements for Valentino's final resting place had still not been made. His coffin was merely moved over one chamber to the spot that had been intended for June Mathis's husband. In a rather macabre twist to this story of haunted hearts, that is exactly where the remains of Rudolph Valentino, the man millions adored, have lain ever since.

While Valentino's body permanently rests in its "temporary" tomb, his spirit is still very active. The young man's darkly handsome image has been seen at the palatial Hollywood home he called Falcon's Lair, at the stables where his favorite horse was kept, at his beach house, in the suite of a hotel he enjoyed visiting, at an apartment building called Valentino Place and in the wardrobe department of Paramount Studios!

But what of the loyal Lady in Black? Her spirit has been equally restless and just as loyal in death as it was in life. Her youthful and formally dressed image is still said to appear each August 23, carrying a bouquet of flowers to the crypt where Rudolph Valentino's body is interred. It's unlikely that the devoted woman's physical body is still alive—she would have to be at least 100 years old by now. Those who have studied this ghost story believe that the mysterious woman died in 1955. Since that year, no one has *heard* the easily identifiable sounds of her high heels clicking along the Cathedral Corridor of the Hollywood Forever Cemetery

Hollywood Forever Cemetery

toward the Great Lover's crypt. People have *seen* her enigmatic image moving silently through the hallway, and at last
report flowers were still being left each year on August 23, the
anniversary of his death.

Even death has not altered this spirit's love and devotion
for Rudolph Valentino.

A Match Waiting Beyond

We've probably all known couples who seem to be an absolutely perfect match—each bringing out the best qualities in the other while shoring up any vulnerabilities that the other possesses. Such a relationship is nothing short of a blessing. Some people believe that everyone has that perfect soul mate somewhere and that it's just a matter of finding that person.

But what if you never have the opportunity to meet that person? What if life hasn't put you and your true love in the same place? Or, as in the case of the following true and carefully documented story, what if life hasn't put the two of you in the same time?

Jan Jones is an intelligent, outgoing woman who holds a responsible position with the police department of a large Canadian city. She has a wide general knowledge and an intense curiosity about the world around her. As Jan has always been a deeply spiritual person, her interest in reincarnation was never a surprise to anyone who knows her. She always assumed that reincarnation was at least part of the explanation for her fascination with the Tudor period of English history because so much specific information about the time came to her in the form of a memory. Some years ago, her feelings of having lived in that time and place were confirmed for Jan under hypnosis.

"I could see the area as clear as a bell. Since then I've found pictures of the place [where I lived]. It looked exactly as I knew it would and that's quite convincing because it is very unique looking. It's a long, low building, which is pretty unusual for a castle," the woman explained.

The *Titanic* is another topic of study that has always fascinated Jan, likely because she has remembered, in this life, having been aboard the ill-fated luxury liner during a previous incarnation. She explained, "The memory presented itself several times, always as falling, falling through darkness. I knew I was dying but I didn't struggle. I just kept thinking to myself, 'This will soon be over.'"

For the past five years Jan has increasingly been drawn to the study of the American Civil War. This passionate interest might not be too surprising if she lived in one of the states involved, but, as a Canadian, the woman's intense curiosity was a bit puzzling—even to Jan herself. Odder still was that the more she delved into the history of the war, the more drawn she felt to investigate the period.

Jan's research led her to photographs taken of various Civil War battle sites, especially those photos that included supernatural "anomalies." Once she viewed these ghostly photos, Jan recognized that she felt a very strong sense of connection to that time and those places. She soon began to realize that these photographs were not just feeding her curiosity, but that they were actually rekindling memories: old memories, very old memories. Memories so old that they were from a previous life!

"As I viewed the photos from the Cedar Creek battle site, I immediately felt a sense of impending danger and I knew that I was worried about someone in particular. I had a great sense of knowing in absolute detail how battles went," Jan related.

Thoroughly intrigued, not only by the subject matter but also by her own powerful emotional reaction to what she was seeing and feeling, Jan continued to probe. She found photographs of some of the soldiers who had fought in those gruesome battles. "When I first came to a photo of Union Army General Horatio Wright, it stopped me right in my tracks. I thought, *I know that man.* I knew him instantly. I recognized him. I had an overwhelming feeling of willingness to follow him anywhere he went. It was very much a feeling of great love."

Although undeniably fascinating and exciting, this revelation was also a bit of a concern to Jan. How could she possibly have known these details? Had she perhaps been a soldier in the Civil War? Jan understood that a soul does not necessarily stay the same sex throughout different incarnations, but the energy she was feeling seemed decidedly feminine to her. If she had lived as a woman during the time of the Civil War, especially a woman who felt an intense love for General Wright, then how could she have known so many details of the battles? Women certainly didn't fight alongside men in that war.

In a strange way, perhaps proving her recovered thought that she would follow Wright anywhere, Jan intensified her research efforts. "I discovered a letter that he had written to his wife. In it, Wright gave extensive details about how a particular battle went. He even wrote of troop numbers and movements. It almost gave the reader a sense of having been there!"

Horatio Wright, the great Civil War hero

It was then that Jan realized why just viewing the photos taken where a battle had been fought had created such intense emotions for her. It also explained why she'd felt that she knew so many details of the deadly skirmishes. The images and words were hauntingly familiar. Jan realized that her soul had not been a Civil War soldier. She had been the recipient of Wright's letter. In a previous incarnation, her soul had lived then and there as Louisa Bradford Wright, General Horatio Wright's beloved wife!

After allowing time for the implications of her discovery to take hold, Jan seemed to feel actual relief, for many details, even seemingly trivial details, now fell into place.

"Over the years, I'd been to psychics for readings. At first they would tell me, 'Oh, yes, you're going to marry and have children,'" Jan recalled. But, as the years went by and it became apparent that she was not going to meet a man she wanted to marry, she realized that those sensitives had merely been telling her what they thought she wanted to hear.

"Finally, I saw a psychic who was honest with me. She said, 'No, I don't see a partner for you in this incarnation.'"

Perhaps feeling both disappointed and yet relieved that the psychic had been honest, Jan continued on with her life. It was many years later that she unearthed the information about General Horatio Wright.

Not long after recognizing her soul's eternal love, Jan was able to arrange an appointment with an especially gifted psychic who was visiting a city near Jan's hometown. "Wright was the first person the psychic mentioned," Jan recalled. "She opened the session by saying 'You've lost your partner, haven't you?' At that time, my mother had just passed away. She and I were very close. She was my mother, yes, but she was also my best friend and so at first that's who I thought the psychic was referring to."

After some discussion between Jan and the psychic, it became clear that the "loss" the woman made reference to was not the grief of having recently lost her mother but a previous loss. Thinking that this gifted medium must have picked up on her past-life relationship with Horatio Wright, Jan volunteered, "We've been together in a previous lifetime." The psychic immediately responded with the statement "You've been together forever."

Jan barely had time to comprehend the impact of the psychic's insight before the woman added, "I can feel so much love from him to you."

Not surprisingly, for a loving couple separated by nearly 150 years, there have been some heartbreaking realities for Jan to deal with. "I have been told on three different occasions that this life is my last incarnation on earth and I'm happy about that. I know that after this life I will finally be reunited with my soul mate and I'm looking forward to that, yet I wouldn't welcome a premature death. There are things I need and want to do and see here before I go on."

Balancing that poignant sentiment is Jan's effervescent sense of humor, as she explains that Wright's soul makes sure she's aware of his presence. "One of his daughters was named Rosa. My mother's name was Rose and, oddly, when Mom died I felt as though I'd lost a child. I moved recently and discovered that I'd chosen a building managed by Key West Property Management. That's a pretty strange name for a company operating on the Canadian Prairies. Louisa and Horatio Wright lived in Key West for 11 years. Also, I've read a letter that Horatio wrote during his years in Key West in which he expressed a strong desire to eat something other than turtle. Interestingly, I have always hated any kind of seafood."

While those inconsequential particulars have been fun for Jan to connect, there have also been more serious issues for her to deal with. "I started collecting Civil War relics, particularly from the battle of Cedar Creek. I felt drawn to that place and those articles but then, whenever I'd touch those relics, I'd get a very worried feeling, as though something bad had happened."

After a bit more investigation, Jan knew what was causing her reaction. General Horatio Wright had been injured in that battle and she, as Louisa, had nursed him back to health. After experiencing a particularly vivid dream of visiting Horatio Wright in an encampment, Jan discovered that Louisa had, in fact, spent a night in camp with her husband. On the night of her dream, Jan had had no idea that wives would occasionally visit the officers.

Jan's unique reality has definitely been difficult for her at times because, although she has a thorough understanding of reincarnation and how it works, she is also acutely aware that we live in a world that does not always accept what it cannot see or touch. "Sometimes it all just seems too 'out there,'" she acknowledged. "There must be something to it, though, when I can even shed some light on Louisa and Wright's relationship for a group of Civil War experts in Virginia. One of the questions that was vexing them was why Wright had been promoted several times and was either immediately demoted or moved laterally. At one point, their close friend Abraham Lincoln stepped in and granted a promotion on the order of the President. The Civil War buffs in Virginia wondered why this happened and happened so often. I was able to explain this to them. The reason was simply that Wright had a Southerner for a wife. Worse, she was from a fairly well-placed Southern family and Wright was not above going that extra mile to help protect her family when the Union army was encamped in their homeland. He also helped several of her cousins who had been captured as spies."

Presumably those connections made Wright slightly suspect to the Union side—a valid explanation for his strange series of lateral moves and outright demotions.

Jan's former-life memories include the family home where Louisa was raised in Culpeper, Virginia. "I do remember it. I have scraps of memories and I knew that there was something very distinctive about the structure. I didn't know what that thing was until I finally saw a photograph of the old house. There was a grain elevator behind it."

After the war, Jan, or rather Louisa as she was known then, and Horatio Wright lived in Washington, D.C. "They enjoyed a privileged life," Jan explained. "By all accounts, Louisa was well liked in Washington society and Horatio was held in high regard as he continued his career as a high-ranking army officer, a veteran of the War of the Rebellion and an honorable man."

In that past lifetime, Horatio predeceased Louisa by two years. Since then, according to a psychic, Louisa's soul has been reincarnated three times, most recently as Jan Jones. Horatio's soul has not returned to this life nor, apparently, will it. His earthly journey ended with his incarnation as General Horatio Wright. Now he waits for Jan's life on this plane to be over so he can be reunited with his true love, his soul mate. Jan lives for that day.

A Tinker's Damn

The stately mansion in Cardiff, Wales, has been gone for well over a century now, replaced by a council house—a very haunted council house. The love story behind that haunting is as poignant as even the most romantic writer could create. Yet it is a true love story—and a true ghost story.

Her name was Kate. His real name has been lost in the mists of time, but it's unimportant anyway, for he went by the nickname "Magpie." That moniker was derived from his habit of always wearing black trousers and jacket and a white vest, reminiscent of the pesky scavenger bird. Magpie was a handsome man, a tinker by trade and a charmer by nature.

As he peddled his wares, calling on the various palatial homes scattered about the country, Magpie would make his way around to the servants' entrance, hoping that a maidservant would answer his knock. He had long ago found that the young women were often favorably affected by his flirtatious ways, whereas a manservant or a higher-ranking woman servant might just send him on his way without so much as a friendly nod. If this tale so far has caused you to wonder whether the scoundrel of a tinker perhaps had more nerve than moral standing, your thoughts would be entirely correct.

Young Kate, it seemed, had not as yet come to that conclusion. She knew only that Magpie's periodic visits to the estate where she worked were the highlights of her dreary life. Naively, she was sure that she was the only woman the devious man ever paid attention to. Once the tinker was sure he had won Miss Kate's affections, he intimated to her that he would think very highly of a girl who would be willing to pass along a bit of her employer's silverware. Soon, Kate's employer began to notice pieces of her silver tea service had gone missing. It was certainly no coincidence that at that very moment Magpie found himself with some extra change jingling in the pockets of his black trousers.

Kate's employers did not have the same happy-go-lucky attitude toward theft as Magpie did—especially when that theft was of their own possessions! They began to keep a close eye on the comings and goings of their household staff. It took only a few days for them to identify their maidservant Kate as the thief. Armed with strong evidence against the girl, they went to the local constabulary. Perhaps further demon-strating her naivete, the young woman was utterly shocked to learn that the family had laid formal charges against her. In due course Kate came before a judge to be tried for the crime of theft. She was found guilty and sentenced—to be hanged.

On the day that the terrified young woman was led up the roughly made stairs of the execution platform, Magpie, who had inspired the crime for which she was about to lose her life, was nowhere to be seen.

Her impending death and the horrible injustice of it all was simply too much for Kate to bear in silence. She shrieked obscenities and threats and curses at the crowd that had gath-ered to watch the terrible spectacle of her execution. As the hangman brought the noose over her hooded head, Kate screamed her last—a prophesy that her employer's house would soon cease to exist. Seconds later, those gathered heard the dreadful sound they had come to hear—the terrible, muf-fled crunching sound that a human neck makes when it breaks. The crowd soon dispersed. Whether they felt that justice had been served or not, they had definitely received the bit of entertainment they had come for.

The estate owners who laid the theft charge against Kate received something more than they had bargained for. The girl's last utterance came true. The mansion where she worked and where the heartless Magpie had plied his devious trade was destroyed. And as recently as 30 years ago, reports from a council house built on the property claimed that the house was haunted—by the ghost of a young maidservant dressed in clothes from the mid-1800s. She may still be searching for an opportunity to give a tinker's damn!

Randy Wraith

"Georgie Porgie, puddin' and pie,
kissed the girls and made them cry.
When the boys came out to play
Georgie Porgie ran away."

Those old nursery rhymes are just nonsense, aren't they? Aren't they? Well, sometimes they are, but did you know that the "Georgie" of "Georgie Porgie" was actually a real person? George Villiers lived in England during the 1600s and was the second Duke of Buckingham. He was also a hard drinker and a ladies' man. Villiers loved the pubs and the wenches who frequented them.

Perhaps his amorous and rambunctious nature also contributed to his eventual disgrace in Parliament. Although we cannot know that for certain, history *is* clear that, at the end of his life here on earth, the man's dying request was that his body be laid to rest at a certain spot in Yorkshire in northern England. Sadly, the duke's plea was ignored and his remains were buried at Westminster Abbey. Villiers' peers may have ended his parliamentary career and disregarded his final wishes, but they couldn't prevent his spirit from carrying on—in more than one sense of that phrase!

Almost immediately after the man's death, patrons at the Cock and Bottle Pub in Yorkshire began to occasionally see a misty image standing near the pub's huge hearth. After downing sufficient spirits to reinforce their courage (or suppress their wisdom, depending on your point of view), these same customers would approach the foggy vision. The closer they got to the image, the less clear it became until, just as they would have been near enough to touch the visitant, it disappeared from sight. Everyone who saw the presence said that it was a tall, nattily dressed man whose hair cascaded past his shoulders.

That description might have matched any number of recently deceased men from the era, but, as the haunting continued, the spirit's personality began to emerge. A woman bathing in a room adjacent to George Villiers' favorite pub recognized the defeated and deceased parliamentarian immediately when he approached her. She screamed a rebuff at the spirit's overtures and the dejected ghost turned away and ascended an attic staircase. The woman's husband came running to see why his wife had screamed. He raced up the same stairs that the ghost had used only moments before. Despite a thorough search, he could not find a soul, living or dead, in the dusty, deserted attic.

Once they'd regained their composure, however, both the husband and his terrified wife realized they were relieved that, at least this time, Georgie Porgie's apparition had kept his hands to himself. They both knew of many females who had been enjoying libations in the pub when they had felt various areas of their bodies being caressed or petted by the randy wraith.

It would seem that, even in death, George Villiers, the second Duke of Buckingham and subject of the "Georgie Porgie" nursery rhyme, still loved to love the ladies!

Doubly Deadly

With the possible exception of the White House, the Octagon is probably the most famously haunted house in Washington, D.C.

When Colonel John Tayloe began to build his family's home in 1799, he knew that it would have to be a large place because he and his wife were the parents of 15 children: seven sons and eight daughters. He also knew that the location of the house would have to be one befitting his social standing. After all, Tayloe was so well connected that President George Washington counted the colonel as one of his closest friends. With all these factors in mind, Tayloe chose an oddly shaped piece of land at the corner of New York Avenue and 18th Street. Perhaps to get the biggest house possible onto the awkward lot, the design he chose was not the standard four-sided building but six-sided, with a dramatic half-round feature as the focal point at the front of the house. Strangely, this six-sided house has always been called the Octagon, a term properly used to refer to an eight-sided structure.

The most striking feature inside the home has always been the elegant rotunda with its enormous, winding oval staircase ascending three stories from the entryway. That grand architectural detail also figures prominently in the most poignant of the ghost stories associated with the house.

Dolley Madison's ghost, which is rumored to haunt the White House, has also been encountered in the Octagon. The phantom footmen seen and heard on the street just outside the house are also linked with the former First Lady. It is likely that these sightings are revenants from the War of 1812. The Madisons lived in the house while workers rebuilt the White House, which had been torched by the British.

The Octagon is probably the second most haunted house in Washington, D.C.

Being forced by the enemy to flee the presidential mansion did nothing to stop Dolley Madison from hosting her famously elegant parties. She continued to entertain lavishly during their temporary residency in the Octagon, which would account not only for her continuing presence, but also for the spirits of the liveried footmen that have apparently never left the place. Once a server, always a server.

But the most poignant ghosts in the stately old home are the spirits of two of Colonel Tayloe's daughters.

The United States and Great Britain were engaged in a bitter war, and Tayloe hated the British. Tragically, one of his beloved daughters fell in love with an officer in the British military. It is said that late one stormy evening, the young woman tried to explain herself to her father, but he would not listen to her entreaties. Frustrated with his lack of compassion, she apparently turned her back to him, picked up a candle from a nearby holder and stormed up the enormous staircase, presumably heading for the privacy of her bedroom.

She never reached her destination. No sooner had the sounds of her feet pounding angrily on the stairs subsided than a scream echoed horribly throughout the house. Seconds later there was a terrible thud and the girl's lifeless body lay in a crumpled heap on the rotunda floor. If anyone ever knew why she had fallen, no one ever said. Was it suicide? Was she just so upset that she stumbled and fell? Had she been pursued by her father? Had there been a struggle? We simply don't know.

Some say the girl's ghost appeared immediately after her fall and that the haunting so tormented her heartsick father that he arranged to have his family move away. Others suggest the move was an escape from the dangers of living in Washington during the war. Whatever the reason or reasons, we do know that once peace was restored and the White House was once again ready for President and Mrs. Madison, the Tayloes resumed residency in the mansion at the corner of New York Avenue and 18th Street.

Perhaps not wanting to risk the possibility that another one of his treasured daughters might choose an inappropriate mate, Colonel Tayloe set about to arrange what he thought would be suitable marriages for the seven remaining girls. When one particular daughter heard about her father's plans, she reacted immediately. The girl followed her heart and fled from her home to elope with the man she loved.

After some period of time, the newly married young woman decided to approach her angry father and ask for his

Footsteps of a woman can be heard running down these stairs.

understanding and acceptance. She paid a visit to the Octagon, but Colonel Tayloe ignored her and, acting as though he didn't even see the girl, started to climb up the massive staircase. Determined to talk to her father, the girl raced up the stairs in pursuit. When she reached him, the man brushed her aside. She lost her balance and, seconds later, died under eerily similar circumstances as her sister. The lavish staircase and John Tayloe's irascible personality had stolen another life.

Since then, every few years, witnesses have reported seeing what looks like the flickering light from a candle ascending the massive, lethal staircase. By now, those familiar with the tale know then to expect to hear a terrible shriek followed by a sickening thud, as history repeats itself over and over again in this agonizingly haunted, oddly shaped and misnamed house.

Eternally Tortured Soul

As the late afternoon shadows lengthened, young Will Robinson hurried across the stately Cambridge campus. He had studied a little too long and was afraid that he might be late meeting his friend Grant Hutchings. Moments later, around a curve in the path and through a stand of trees, Will was gratified and relieved to catch a glimpse of Grant making his way toward him.

I'm not that late after all, Robinson realized with a smile. *But I wonder who that man is walking just a little behind Grant. The guy looks old enough to be one of our profs, but I've sure never seen him before. Weird that he's walking so close to Grant but not beside him. Oh well, I'll find out in a minute, I guess.*

As Robinson and Hutchings came closer to one another, each man called out a greeting and waved. *Funny,* Robinson thought, *that old guy didn't even look up. Maybe he's deaf or something. I wonder who he is.*

Seconds later, Grant Hutchings, the more flamboyant of the two friends, reached out his hand to give Will Robinson a friendly pat on the back.

"How are you?" Robinson asked. "I'm glad I didn't keep you waiting. I was afraid I would. That trigonometry really has me stumped this year."

"Funny, I thought I'd kept you waiting," Hutchings replied before beginning to complain about a class they had both attended earlier in the day.

The enjoyment of being out of doors, away from the pressures of studies and with his effervescent friend, caused Will Robinson to forget for a few moments that he had seen a strange man walking almost beside Grant. As soon as he remembered, Robinson took advantage of the first pause in Hutchings' chatter to inquire.

"Where'd that man go? The one who was just about beside you as you were walking around that curve in the path by the grove of trees," Will inquired.

"No one was anywhere near me. As a matter of fact, I didn't see anyone—not a soul from the time I left the dormitory till I saw you walking toward me," Grant replied with a puzzled tone in his voice.

"You're putting me on, Hutchings," Robinson countered, emphasizing his point by stopping and turning to face his friend. "I saw someone with you. He wasn't walking quite beside you. It was as if he couldn't quite keep up with you because he was always a half step behind. He was an older man, well dressed. He had such a graceful gait that he almost seemed to float rather than walk over the path. You can't tell me that you didn't know he was there. He was so close to you that your shoulders were almost touching."

Grant Hutchings was quiet for a moment. Suddenly he understood exactly what had happened. Oddly, he'd had the sense that someone had been near him, but he'd been so pre-occupied with thoughts of his classes and being late to meet his friend, he'd just dismissed the feeling. Now there could be no denying what must have happened. He had been visited by the campus ghost.

"Have you ever heard the rumor that this campus is haunt-ed?" Grant asked his friend as they slowly began to walk again.

A strange look darted across Robinson's face as he shook his head.

"I'm surprised you haven't. Legend has it that there is a ghost on this part of the grounds. They say it's been haunted for nearly 200 years. It all started in the early 1800s, around 1820, I think. If you'd like, I can tell you the story the way it was told to me."

Will's only reply was a slight nod of his head.

Grant began to recount the legend.

The ghost is the specter of a man named Christopher Round. He was a student at Cambridge in the early 1800s. He lived to a ripe old age but, when he did die, his spirit came back because his soul is eternally tormented by a fatal judgment error he made when he was at school.

Round was a serious young man who kept to himself, worked extremely hard and excelled in his studies. Most of his fellow students knew him, at least by his reputation as an exceptional student, but because he didn't take part in any of the usual extracurricular college activities, no one on campus really counted Christopher Round as their friend. He was just present, sitting with them day after day in classes. After exams, when the marks were posted, they would see his name well above theirs on the rankings. Well, his name was above *most* of the others. One student, Philip Collier, consistently bested Round's marks. Not only that, but Collier also excelled in athletics, served on almost every student committee, danced with exquisite grace, played a mean hand of bridge and was a thoroughly nice, considerate and helpful person.

It was Collier who, along about the middle of second year, first noticed that the studious young Christopher Round's personality was lightening up a bit. Why, occasionally Christopher almost seemed happy. Of course, it wasn't long before other students also noticed the improvement in his disposition, and soon whispers about the possible cause began to circulate. Collier was the only one brash enough to come right out and ask Christopher about it. He just wasn't ready for the reply he received.

Christopher Round was an introverted student, so the answer he gave Collier was quite surprising. Of course, young men have been falling happily in love since time began but, because Round had never shown much interest in anything beyond academics, the news that he had been smitten by a beautiful woman was quite a shock. More disconcerting still was the object of his affections—the recently widowed Lady Mary Clifford. Round had met the distraught woman through the office where he worked part-time as a clerk. He had been assigned to help her with the reams of inevitable paperwork she had encountered after her husband's unexpected death.

Over the course of their business meetings, Round became more and more infatuated with Lady Clifford until finally he announced, to himself, that he was in love with the young widow. Thus brightened by love, Christopher Round had struck his fellow students as being unlike his former self.

Some weeks after their first meeting, Lady Clifford announced that she was going abroad on an extended vacation to fully recover from her grief. Round's heart sank at the news. He had hoped that before too long he might find an opportunity to ask the widow if she would do him the honor of dining with him. Soon, however, the smitten Christopher was able to console himself with the thought that his beloved would be back before the year was out. Besides, he had his studies to distract him and keep him busy, especially as Philip Collier had unexpectedly withdrawn from the university for the term. Round now had the chance to enjoy the satisfaction of achieving the highest marks in every class he was attending.

Despite his best efforts to keep his mind on his studies, over the months that Lady Clifford was away Christopher Round often found his thoughts drifting toward her and even toward the possibility of a future together. It was unusual, he knew, to find a woman as serious and intense as Mary was, and, given his own personality, those were characteristics Round held in great esteem.

As the weeks turned to months and the date for Lady Clifford's return neared, Christopher became more and more excited. In the time she'd been away, the young man had built a complex fantasy of their loving future together as husband and wife. All that was left now, he was sure, was for them to live out his dream. When the day finally came that he first saw her again, Round was more convinced than ever that their story would have a "happily ever after" ending. He was so committed to making his fantasy a reality that he barely even reacted when Mary told him about the amazing coincidence that had occurred while she was resting in an Italian villa. It seemed that a "friend" of his, Philip Collier, had also been vacationing there and the two had enjoyed many interesting hours in one another's company.

Although Christopher was eager to spend time with the lady, he decided to pay her the courtesy of waiting a few days before asking her out. On each and every one of those days, as he made his way across the campus from one lecture to another, Christopher Round overheard at least one conversation about the obvious love affair going on between Lady Mary Clifford and Philip Collier. Soon it became clear to Christopher that the solemn nature he thought he'd detected and had so greatly admired in Mary had not been that at all. The introspection that he had seen had merely been temporary melancholy, a product of her grief. Apparently, the combination of time and Collier's attentions had revived her fun-loving, frivolous nature—and Christopher had once again been edged out by his rival.

As sad as he was, Christopher Round came to realize that there was no way he and Lady Mary could have had the life he'd dreamed of. Their personalities were not as close a match as he had initially thought. Still, he cared deeply for the woman and, in his heart, wished her only happiness. That was why Round was horrified the night he found Philip Collier so obviously very drunk. Upset at the implications of Collier's drunkenness, Round set out for a long walk through the darkened campus and on to the nearby riverbank. He walked for hours and hours—throughout most of the night—until finally he felt calm enough to return to his room and, although it was nearly dawn, get a bit of sleep.

When he awoke, the troubled young man realized that his walk had rejuvenated his soul, so he developed a habit of taking long walks late every evening. And that was how, days later, he came to be at the side of the river in time to see Collier on the bank not far upstream. Judging from the other man's staggering gait, Christopher guessed that Philip was drunk once again and had come outside to walk off the effects of too much alcohol.

Round stood and stared in dismay at the scene before him. All the tormented emotions that he thought he'd rid himself of came flooding back to assault him. By the time he heard the screams, Round was so sickened with confusion that he actually wondered if he himself had cried out. It wasn't until he saw the splash of water come up from the edge of the river that Christopher Round realized what had happened. Collier had been so inebriated that he had fallen from the riverbank into the water.

Serves him right, Round thought. *Besides, Collier's a good swimmer, just like he's good at everything else. Even if he's drunk, he's not going to come to any harm in the water.* And, with that thought, Round turned and walked away.

The next morning, Christopher was surprised to learn that all classes had been cancelled for the day. The entire campus— students and faculty alike—was in mourning. While taking a walk at sunrise, a professor had spotted a body floating face down in the river. Without a thought to his own well-being, the man had waded out into the water to see if perhaps he was still in time to help. When he managed to turn the person over, he realized he had found the body of one of Cambridge's most popular and successful students—Philip Collier.

Like most of his fellow students, Christopher Round was shocked and saddened by the news, but, unlike the others, Christopher also felt deeply guilty. He could have—he should have—pulled the struggling man out of the river. After all, he had seen Collier fall into the water, and deep down he had really known, despite his rationalizations, that the man was in no condition to save himself. Round might not have *killed* his longtime rival but, by his grave sin of omission, had in fact allowed Collier to die. Badly shaken by this dreadful turn of events, Round became even more withdrawn and reclusive than he was before. And that is why it took several weeks for the additional bits of information to filter through to Round's guilty consciousness.

Philip Collier had not been drunk when Round had seen him by the river. Nor had Collier been drunk the previous time Round had seen him acting strangely. To earn extra money, Collier had volunteered to be part of an experiment that medical students on campus were carrying out to determine the best dosage of a new type of anesthetic. Instead of wasting time and money on drinking, the young man had in fact been acting completely in character—by doing more than other students and perhaps contributing to the betterment of other people's lives. It was the aftereffects of the new anesthetic, not alcohol, that had caused Philip Collier to stumble around as if he were drunk.

No charges were ever laid in connection with the terrible tragedy. Christopher Round never confessed to anyone that he had witnessed the fall or that he probably could have prevented Philip Collier's death if he had been able to overcome his selfish anger and pain. But Round did not go unpunished. He had lost, indeed never had, the love of Lady Mary Clifford. And, for the rest of his long life, this sensitive and philosophical man's essence was tortured by the knowledge that his own inaction had allowed another man's premature death.

We know that it is *his* ghost that is occasionally seen on the imposing old grounds of Cambridge, because it seems that Round didn't quite take his secret to his grave. Less than a year before his death, the tortured man wrote a detailed account of the terrible events that had taken place so very long ago. Then he placed the document into a sturdy envelope and sealed it closed with candle wax drippings. He handed the envelope to a young man whom he admired, with instructions that the contents were not to be read until 50 years after Round's death.

By the time that date finally arrived, Lady Mary Clifford, Philip Collier and even Christopher Round had been all but forgotten. Until then, no one who walked the grounds of the

University of Cambridge late at night knew the story of the ghost they would see every now and then.

When Grant Hutchings had finished telling this tale there was a moment of silence between him and Will Robinson, for then they both knew that it was this same haunted heart, the ghost of Christopher Round, that Will had seen walking just behind his friend.

And, as far as anyone knows, on cloudless nights when a full moon shines brightly and dances across the river's surface near the wooden walking path, poor Christopher Round's tormented, lovesick soul can still be seen.

Eduardo's Evil Family

Although an American by birth, Angela was living in Paris in 1945. She joined everyone in the French city in relief and happiness when the war finally ended. But Angela had an additional reason for happiness. She was in love—with a handsome, charming Spanish nobleman whom we shall call Eduardo.

The couple would already have married if it hadn't been for the man's wealthy family. They insisted that he marry a woman of their choosing and, because they managed much of his money, they were in a position to make his life very difficult if he chose to ignore their wishes. After much thought and discussion, however, Eduardo and Angela went ahead with plans for their own small wedding.

For their honeymoon, the newlyweds traveled to Spain, hoping for at least a politely tolerant reception from Eduardo's parents. Those hopes were quickly and soundly dashed, for his parents did nothing to hide their disapproval of Angela. Hurt and angry, the couple left his parents' home almost immediately.

The bride had barely recovered from her in-laws' rudeness when the unthinkable occurred—her beloved husband suffered a massive heart attack and died instantly. Now, in addition to her vengeful in-laws, Angela had to deal with all-encompassing grief as she tried to arrange for her beloved's funeral. It didn't take long for the young widow to realize that her husband's family was not just wealthy, but also very influential. Everywhere she turned, people made it clear to Angela that they would not support her in any way.

The family's callousness knew no bounds. To prevent the grieving woman from inheriting what was rightfully hers, they set about having their son's marriage annulled. Dejected, alone and almost poverty-stricken, Angela fled from the Continent to stay with a friend in London.

After allowing Angela a few days of complete rest, the friend wondered if some visitors would distract the woman from her troubles and perhaps help to lift her spirits. Angela's hostess arranged for her neighbor Loretta to come for afternoon tea. The three women were making quiet, and rather meaningless, conversation when suddenly Loretta's demeanor stiffened.

"I don't usually mention this, because sometimes people react strangely," the visitor began in a strained voice. "But sometimes I am sensitive to those who have already passed to the next life and I must tell you, Angela, that there is a man standing directly behind you."

The color drained from Angela's face and, for a moment, her friend was afraid that she might fall into a dead faint.

The psychic continued, "He's a handsome man who has recently passed into the afterlife. He's trying to get a message to you, but I can't make out what it is he wants to say. When I was younger, I had some luck communicating with spirits by automatic writing. If you get me a pen and some paper, I'll see if his message will come through that way."

Silently, the hostess handed Loretta the writing tools she had requested. Seconds later, the only sound in the room was the sound of the nib of a pen scratching across a page. Angela and her friend barely dared to breathe as they watched Loretta with her head flung back, clearly in a trance, frenetically writing.

A few moments later, with a loud exhalation, Loretta dropped the pen and jolted from her trance back into consciousness.

She took a deep breath before handing the sheet of paper, now covered with words, to Angela's outstretched hand.

Anxiously, Angela examined the document. After a moment, her eyes filled with tears and, choking back sobs, she told the other two women, "This means nothing to me. There are some numbers here, a man's name and an address in Paris."

"Let me see that," Angela's friend said, grabbing at the paper. "If this information is from the soul of your departed husband, then it must mean something. This first number is a telephone number. I'm going to call it and ask for the man whose name is on the sheet."

Moments later, Angela and her friend knew for certain that the neighbor was psychic. The mystery was solved. The man whose number they called had known Angela's husband. The address was for a bank in Paris and the numbers were a code required to open a safe-deposit box.

Angela said her good-byes and left for France the very next day. She lost no time in finding the bank and accessing the locked metal storage drawer that her husband had apparently rented. What she found hidden there could not have shocked her more! A letter from her late husband lay on top. In it, he explained that he had known his health was not the best, even when he married Angela, and he also knew that, when he died, his greedy family would not treat her well. Under the letter lay a substantial stack of money, and on the bottom, among a few exquisite pieces of fine jewelry, lay a set of car keys on a fob bearing the address of a nearby garage.

Barely able to comprehend what was happening to her, Angela left the bank and walked to the garage, where she was told that she held keys to a sports car that had been stored there for some months. Inside the car's trunk, the woman found even more cash. Her beloved husband had managed to provide for her, despite his cruel family's best, or worst, intentions.

Angela immediately arranged to sail home to America—her new sports car in the ship's cargo hold. She was able to start a small business with the money that her husband had left for her. And, although she never remarried, the widow lived a long, happy and satisfying life that would not have been possible if it hadn't been for a message from a ghost.

Carolina Love Story

The Carolinas' coastlines are positively alive with ghosts and ghost stories. Over the centuries, as the Atlantic Ocean has crashed against these shores, it has taken many souls into its watery grave. Some of the resulting stories have become so entrenched in the local culture that they have become legendary. Almost every lighthouse worth its Fresnel lens, for instance, has at least one ghost story associated with it. In addition, haunted houses dot the mainland and ghost lights shine mysteriously on many of the islands. Even Edward Teach, the most treacherous pirate ever to sail the seven seas, left ghost stories involving the Carolinas in his wake. (If you're wondering why that name isn't familiar to you, it's probably because the villain has always been best known by the name Blackbeard.)

Although many of the details have been lost in the mists of time, one of the most tragic ghostly legends from the shores of the Carolinas is a love story. The tale began when a certain ship docked at the port town where a young woman we'll call Susanna lived with her wealthy parents. The girl had been born and raised in the town and she'd been promised in marriage to a neighboring family's son, so it was likely she would die there. Most young lasses of that day would accept such a destiny as simply inevitable.

But Susanna was not like most of the others. She longed to travel, to see the world. If she couldn't do that, then she at least wanted to hear tales from someone who did. Perhaps this is why, when she was passing the docks one day, she smiled back at a handsome young sailor who had smiled at her.

Taken by the sailor's friendly manner, Susanna just "happened" to stroll to the docks again the very next day. She was delighted to see that the same ship was still there. Better still, the young sailor himself was sitting on the wharf, almost as though he'd been waiting for Susanna. Of course, attractive young people being what they are, the two soon introduced themselves and were chatting happily. Susanna was enthralled by Arthur's seafaring tales of lands far away. The two made arrangements to meet again the next day—and the next and the next and the next. When the sad day finally came that he had to leave for another voyage, he did so with a promise that he would return.

Susanna's family, in the meantime, was busy making plans for her wedding, which was scheduled for the following summer. Over the winter, the young woman lived her life as though in a daze. All she could think of was how happy she would be to see her beloved sailor again and to hear more about his adventures.

Finally, spring arrived, and with it the young man's ship. Susanna rushed to the dock. As the deckhands anchored the vessel, Arthur waved to her from the ship's railing. Susanna felt as though her heart would burst. When he finally came ashore, the two embraced passionately and immediately declared their feelings of love for one another.

"My parents have already promised my hand in marriage. I don't love him, though. He's a boring banker," Susanna declared. "You and I will just have to run away together."

The sailor nodded thoughtfully before telling her, "My ship is leaving again tomorrow, but I will be back in the summer. Let's make plans for then."

Susanna waited patiently for her sailor to return.

With their pact set, the two said good-bye. Susanna went along with all the plans for her wedding to the town's banker so as not to raise suspicion. They were to be married in mid-August. The bride-to-be was sure that by that time she would already be wed—to Arthur—and that the two of them would be sailing off together to lives filled with romance and adventure.

But when summer came, there was no sign of the ship that Susanna was so anxious to see. She was frantic with worry, afraid that something terrible had happened. Every summer morning the first thing she did was hurry to the docks to see if his ship had finally come in—even on the day she was to be married! Dressed in her wedding gown, soon to marry another, Susanna rejoiced as she at last spotted the ship carrying her true love.

As the sailors from his ship began to emerge, Susanna stood on tiptoes watching eagerly for her man. When she finally saw him, though, the moment was certainly not the special one that she had been hoping for. You see, a beautiful girl clung to Arthur's arm! Worse, the two were smiling happily at one another, oblivious to the world around them. Susanna was devastated. She fainted dead away and fell into the water beside the dock.

Fortunately, her brother, who had been searching all over town for her, saw what happened. He ran to the end of the dock, dove into the water and pulled the young woman from the bottom where her heavy bridal gown had pulled her. He had saved Susanna's life, but it's doubtful that she ever thanked him for his heroics.

By the time she had recovered from her faint and near-drowning, word of the catastrophe had spread throughout the town. Gossips' tongues began to wag. Susanna's earlier rendezvous with the sailor had not gone unnoticed. When the banker groom-to-be heard the stories, he called off the wedding.

Susanna's brother was furious when he learned the full story. After all, his sister had not only made a laughingstock of the family but had nearly died in her wedding gown because of some scoundrel sailor. Armed with a pistol, the brother boarded the sailor's ship, found the rogue and fired a single, fatal shot to the young man's head. Susanna's heart was broken into even smaller pieces.

For days all the distraught Susanna could do was sit on the porch of her parents' home, staring vacantly into space.

And that is exactly what she was doing when a familiar-looking girl walked toward her. It was none other than the woman who'd clung to her beloved's arm that fateful day!

"Go away!" Susanna cried, but the woman didn't slow her pace. She was determined to speak to Susanna.

"You must listen to what I have to say," the young woman began. "I am grieving, too. The sailor you were in love with was my brother. He asked me to meet him that day and to act as though we were lovers. He knew that you had fallen in love with him and he loved you—enough that he wanted you to have more than what he, a poor sailor, could provide. He thought that if you saw him carrying on with someone else that you would forget him and marry the man he thought you deserved; the man your parents had chosen for you."

Instantly, Susanna's mere heartbreak descended into utter and complete insanity. From that day forward, she never drew a sane breath. Townsfolk would often see her in a tattered old bridal gown, wandering aimlessly along the shore and the docks. Susanna's life had been completely ruined.

Ah, but her afterlife! It must have been wonderful because, for years, as the living watched in awe, two ghosts—one wearing a white gown and the other an old-fashioned sailor's uniform—strolled hand-in-hand near the docks in that haunted town.

Does She or Doesn't She?

New Orleans, Louisiana, could well hold bragging rights as the most haunted place in the United States of America. The very fabric of the city's social history is interwoven with eerie supernatural tales. Some of those stories are ghost stories, and some of those ghost stories are also love stories. The following legend is one of those—a ghost story about love—in this case, the kind of love money can buy.

Josie Arlington was, not to put too fine a point on it, a madam. That didn't mean she was a criminal. Josie operated her house of ill repute during the early 1900s, when prostitution in New Orleans had temporarily been legalized. Of course, just because Josie's business was legal didn't make it respectable, and so the wives of her wealthy patrons snubbed the madam completely.

Josie didn't much care. In her estimation, she had more than they did, anyway. Not only did she have the respect and sometimes the love of their husbands, but she also had a business that provided her with an extremely comfortable life. Of course life, no matter how comfortable, is fleeting. Death, on the other hand, lasts forever.

Perhaps that is why Josie chose the graveyard as the perfect place from which to seek revenge against those who had scorned her. First, she carefully selected a plot in the city's most prestigious cemetery. Then, just as carefully, she chose an artisan to create an ornate red marble tomb to hold her earthly remains. As a finishing touch, Josie commissioned a life-sized statue of a woman carrying a bouquet of roses. The statue was to be placed facing the tomb, thereby forever turning its back on the other, more respectable, occupants of the cemetery while also forever welcoming Josie with the flowers symbolizing a gift of love. These monuments were paid for with the money earned from her wealthy and affectionate patrons. She was apparently not one for subtle messages!

Josie's masterpiece of revenge was completed in 1911, a few years before she died. Not long after the grave markings had been erected, passersby began to notice that, on moonlit nights, the red marble tomb looked eerily as though it were on fire. Some even said it resembled the way they had always imagined the Gates of Hell might look. No one was comfortable with anything about the monument; no one, that is, except Josie. She was delighted.

In 1914, when the former madam did pass on to her final reward, her gravesite began to draw even more attention. People, even workers in the cemetery, were sure that the statue facing the tomb occasionally moved. It was as though the sculpture had, upon the madam's death, been imbued with life. A report from two graveyard caretakers indicated that they watched the statue leave its post and wander about the other graves before suddenly disappearing. Although their whimsical story was and is highly suspect, the tales about Josie's tomb became entrenched in the city's folklore. Most people considered the anecdotes to be rather intriguing and amusing.

To Henri Gandalfo, who worked at the cemetery for decades and in 1981 published a memoir about it, these supernatural stories were nothing but nonsense. Gandalfo maintained that sightings of the flames stopped as soon as a particular streetlight was removed in the 1920s, and, as for the statue moving, the historian simply couldn't or wouldn't credit that at all. He was sure that there was nothing of a paranormal nature at work, and insisted that people were seeing and believing only what they wanted to see and believe.

And, of course, he might be right. Josie's revenge might have been complete the moment her earthly remains were laid to rest in her carefully chosen and designed final resting place. Or, perhaps, it is just as possible that the skeptical Gandalfo was also guilty of seeing and believing only what he wanted to see and believe. In the end, we simply don't know. Does the ghost of one of New Orleans' most loved madams haunt her own tomb, enjoying eternal revenge—or doesn't she?

A Capital Haunt

The old home is gone now, torn down years ago. It's really a shame because, even though it wasn't a mansion, it *was* once a grand old place. By the time it was demolished in the early 1900s, the two-story house was little more than a crumbling ruin. No one, except the odd squatter and an assortment of varmints, had lived in it for years.

Oh, many people had tried to call the place home. After all, it was spacious and even still held glimmers of its former elegance; moreover, the resale price was always considerably less than that of any other house in the prestigious Georgetown, Washington, D.C., neighborhood. Despite all this, neither bargain hunters nor status seekers could stay in the place for more than a few weeks. You see, this house was decidedly haunted.

The first family to try living in the place after the original tenant had departed was puzzled to note that the cleanest part of the house was the staircase landing between the first and second stories. At the time, they didn't think much of it and simply set about making the rest of their new home as clean as that four-square-foot spot. Once they had the house sparkling clean, they were most pleased with its appearance. They weren't, however, pleased with the atmosphere in it. Often, just at dusk, they noticed strange rustling sounds that seemed to travel from the front door of the house to the staircase. Perhaps because of those mysterious noises, perhaps for other reasons, they soon sold the dwelling and moved on, without bothering to advise the new owners of the inexplicable sounds they'd sometimes heard in the home.

The next family to move in also heard those evening noises, but they described them as "swishing" sounds. They also noted that accompanying the sound was a strange cool breeze or draft that would always swirl from the front door and up the staircase to the first landing. In addition to that oddity, they confided to a few friends that for some unknown reason they were never really able to warm to the place, to feel at home. Then, just as they were preparing to move out, their son caught a glimpse of something very strange.

The young man had been about to go upstairs to rest when he felt a familiar, but still decidedly uncomfortable, chill develop in the air around him. He shrugged his shoulders in a vain attempt to shake off the unpleasant prickly sensation that the mysterious draft always gave him. Still feeling ill at ease, he looked around. What that lad saw became a memory he took to his grave. There, moving toward him, was a vaporous formation about the size and shape of a small human being, at least smaller than he was. Worse, this strange mist was moving—not walking, but floating just a bit above the floor. As the form moved, the air around the young man became even cooler, as if the misty being was bringing cold air with it.

The youngster was the first and only member of the family to have seen and identified the reason that they had never been able to make their lovely house a home. They had been sharing the premises with a ghost!

Badly shaken by his encounter, the young man leaned against the newel at the bottom of the staircase and watched the ghost drift up toward the second floor. But before the image reached the landing, the mist dispersed and the air warmed. The spirit had disappeared, temporarily. The lad was sure it would be back, over and over again, as the tortured soul replayed those particular moments of life—and death.

After taking a moment to compose himself, the young man continued up the stairs. He'd already decided not to say anything to his parents until they had actually moved out of the house. It seemed pointless to disturb them any more than they already were. And so, the owners vacated the house without realizing they had been trying to share their space with a tormented soul doomed to relive her most horrid last few moments on this plane. Once their son told them what he had seen, it wasn't long before the story made the newspapers. From then on, the once fine-looking house stood empty more often than occupied until it became home only to the occasional squatter, host of insects and family of rodents. Eventually, much to the relief of the neighbors, the place was torn down.

By that time, the politician who had long ago owned the house had also died. Sadly for his posthumous reputation, however, he did not completely succeed in taking the story of an illicit love affair to the grave with him. It was that dirty little secret that solves the mystery of a haunted house in Georgetown, Washington, D.C.

With the dawning of the 19th century, a certain Southern belle decided that she was thoroughly fed up with her mundane life—a life that included the boring man she was soon to marry. Not one to sit idly by, the young woman took immediate, if unwise, action. She seduced one of the slaves on her family's plantation estate. As bad luck would have it, the girl's father stumbled upon the spot the pair had chosen for their tryst. Moments later, the worker lay dead and the belle was being dragged, kicking and screaming, back to the main house.

Word of the disgrace spread through the community like lightning. The lovely, if indiscreet, young lady had tarnished not only her own family's name but also that of the young man she was betrothed to. There was no question in her mind; the familiar, privileged life she had been raised in was over. Her only option was to adopt a new life as quickly and as drastically as she possibly could.

And so that evening, under cover of darkness, the young lady slipped away from the estate she had always called home and made her way to the stagecoach office in the nearest town. Without bothering to ask what its destination might be, she bought a one-way ticket for the next coach scheduled to leave. An hour later, the runaway found herself sitting next to a middle-aged man, a politician by profession. It was only then that she realized the stagecoach was bound for the new nation's capital.

During the long and uncomfortable journey, the politician and the young lady became quite interested in each other, although for very different reasons. He thought she could provide him with an attractive and impressive companion, and she thought he could provide her with various kinds of support.

Happily, the two were able to accommodate one another. Soon the politician was frequently seen arriving to visit the pretty lady at the splendid new residence he had secretly bought for her in Georgetown, then a separate city near the capital.

But our gal was not content just to spend her days waiting for her sugar daddy to visit. Before long, she was casting about for a business opportunity to become involved in. After some thought, the former Southern belle realized that she didn't even need to leave home to expand her horizons. She could and would open an exclusive brothel right there in the posh Georgetown home that her "friend" had bought for her.

Meanwhile, back at the plantation, the girl's former fiancé had also been doing some thinking. Unfortunately, he was fixing to find his once bride-to-be and to let her know just how heartily unhappy he was with her past indiscretions. After making as many general inquiries as he could, the fellow began hearing about a madam in Washington, D.C., who bore an uncanny resemblance to the young woman who used to be his betrothed. He decided to make his way north to check out this "coincidence."

When he found the prestigious address, the man wasted no time in confirming the rumors he had heard. He knocked on the door of the brothel and, seconds later, the former couple was face to face once again. Well, almost. It was really his pistol that the girl saw most clearly, for it was pointed directly at a spot between her eyes.

The woman shrieked in terror and ran into the house. As she reached the bottom of the staircase that led to the bedrooms, she gathered up the skirts and petticoats of her floor-length dress and bolted up the stairs two at a time. The girl's efforts were in vain, for she had no sooner reached the landing than the sound of a pistol shot rang out. She barely had time to summon a scream before her lifeless body collapsed on the landing.

Her spirit, however, stayed on in the house for over 100 years. And as we saw earlier, anyone who lived in that home after the murder often heard the rustling of skirts swishing about the entranceway and even ascending the stairs to the first landing leading to the bedrooms.

A newspaper article from the 1800s mentions that, while listening to the phantom sounds, a reliable witness had sighted a shadowy form moving from room to room in the lovely old place.

When the house of illicit love was torn down, perhaps the girl's restless spirit found the peace in her eternity that she lacked in her lifetime.

The Irish Hitcher

Phantom hitchhiker stories are found as often in anthologies of urban legends as in ghost story collections. These tales tend to be rather vague, often lacking details of where and when the encounter with the phantom actually occurred. Perhaps the missing details are what give such stories so many similarities.

While this tale definitely fits into the phantom hitchhiker category, it is different from most others. The specifics have been so well preserved that the account, presented in the media as being factual, is unusually believable. The report was published in *Beyond* in April 1969 and indicates that these events took place the previous February. The haunted stretch of road lies between Ballyporeen and Tipperary, Ireland, and the phantom hitchhiker is the soul of one Brigit O'Terrell.

But before a person can appreciate this poignant ghost story, one must know its tragic history.

In 1955, Brigit O'Terrell, while mourning the loss of her beloved husband, received word that her married daughter was seriously ill with blood poisoning. She had been taken to a hospital in Tipperary, near where the younger woman and her husband made their home. Terrified at the prospect of losing her only daughter without at least saying a proper farewell, Mrs. O'Terrell fled from her tiny house in the south-central village of Clogheen to the highway leading to Tipperary.

When she saw a car approach, the nearly hysterical woman ran to the middle of the road and began waving her arms madly about. Barely waiting for the vehicle to come to a complete stop, Brigit frantically pulled open its passenger's door and all but ordered the shocked driver to take her to the hospital in Tipperary. The driver complied immediately and, even though it was raining and road conditions were poor, their trip went well for nearly 10 miles. As they approached a crossroads near a farm owned by a man named Duncan, the car was hit head-on by another vehicle. Both Brigit and the Good Samaritan driver whose car she had commandeered were killed instantly. Widow O'Terrell and her dying daughter, who lived only a few hours longer than her mother did, were denied their last good-byes.

Since then, Mrs. O'Terrell's ghost has made that same futile journey at least twice, leaving two extremely convincing, heart-wrenching stories of encounters with a special phantom hitchhiker on a never-ending mission.

In February 1969, Charles Halloran was driving to Cork in southwestern Ireland. Charles traveled a great deal on business and always made a point, for safety's sake, never to pick up hitchhikers. On this day, he felt compelled to make an exception to his own rule. After all, the woman he saw on the road ahead was clearly not an ordinary hitchhiker. She was frantically waving her arms in the air. It was clear that she was in serious distress.

Almost before Halloran had braked to a complete stop, the frenzied woman jumped into the passenger's seat beside him. "You must take me to Tipperary," she commanded, before explaining that a messenger had just brought word that her daughter was gravely ill and had been taken to the hospital there.

Although Mr. Halloran knew where Tipperary was, he was not familiar with the route and so told his distraught passenger that she would have to give him specific directions. Between heart-wrenching sobs, Brigit agreed to do her best.

For miles, the pair drove along in virtual silence, the only sound being the woman's uncontrolled cries. For his part, Charles Halloran was pleased not to have to make conversation. For some reason that he did not quite understand, he was feeling extremely uncomfortable, almost to the point of panic. Helping this woman was exacting an enormous emotional cost from him. He felt chilled to the bone and so anxious that he almost felt ill.

As the pair in the car approached a crossroads near a farm owned by a man named Duncan, Brigit O'Terrell suddenly shouted at Halloran, "Don't go through that intersection! Turn here instead."

As Halloran made the turn, he felt his tension increase even further—for the woman was now leading him away from Tipperary. Despite actually feeling afraid of this strange stranger by now, he knew he'd have to speak up. "That road goes in the wrong direction," he told her, making an effort to keep his voice from quavering.

"Hush," Brigit O'Terrell screamed at the man. "Just do as I say or we'll both die."

Halloran's fear was mounting. He confessed later that he had lost all concept of time and felt that the misadventure was beginning to seem like a waking nightmare. With each passing mile, the woman sitting next to him was becoming more and more disturbed and, no matter how hard he tried not to, Charles Halloran found that he was taking on her tension. He was filled with relief when they finally arrived at the hospital in Tipperary.

Brigit fled from the car without so much as a bye-your-leave or even a well-deserved word of thanks to Halloran. He wasn't worried about her lack of niceties, though. He was glad to be free of the terrible responsibility that had been imposed on him, and, for a minute, he just sat quietly letting a feeling of relief wash over him and assuring himself that his dreadful experience was finally at an end.

After a few moments, the man realized that it would be impolite to drive off not knowing if the woman had a way of getting back home or even if her daughter had lived or died. With a sigh, he left the refuge of his car and went into the hospital to make appropriate inquiries.

If Charles Halloran was hoping the hospital receptionist might advise him that Brigit O'Terrell's daughter was doing well and that Brigit's son-in-law would be taking the widow home, he had an eerie surprise coming. The pleasant woman behind the reception counter didn't, at first, have any idea whom Halloran was referring to. After some thought, however, she knew exactly whom he meant and what had happened. She had quite a story to tell the hapless driver, who listened in stunned silence.

It seems that the receptionist had heard almost exactly the same story only a few weeks before. In that earlier case, it had been three men in a car who had stopped for the same frantic woman on the same country road. While Halloran had never heard this particular phantom hitchhiker story, all three men in the other car were well familiar with the bit of folklore. They reported that the woman had appeared so life-like to them that they were convinced she was nothing but a practical joker who had been set up to make fools of them. Imagine their surprise when the atmosphere in the vehicle became as cold and tense as Halloran had also described. This trio even went so far as to say that, while the distraught woman's ghost was riding with them, they seemed to have been somehow under her control. As with Halloran's trip, theirs also ended with the woman disappearing as she reached the front door of the hospital in Tipperary. The trio had certainly not been the butt of a practical joke. They, along with Halloran, had encountered a ghost on her last mission—a mission of the heart.

Although the theory hasn't yet been proven, some locals believe that at least once a year, this phantom hitchhiker reenacts the journey that was cut off by tragedy before she could reach the bedside of her beloved, dying daughter.

A Kiss Is Just a Kiss

When is a kiss not just a kiss? Apparently the answer to that question lay in Greenfield, Ohio, just before Valentine's Day in 1881.

Tucked beside the classified ads for "Situations Wanted" and "Situations Offered" in the *Toronto Daily Mail's* February 11, 1881, edition is an unusual article. Credited to the *New York Times,* its headline reads, "An Osculatory Ghost: The Young Men of an Ohio Town Terrified by a Spectre Given to Kissing."

The nameless scribe who penned the news story opened by assuring readers that the facts stated in the headline were absolutely true. "Greenfield, Ohio, has a real ghost. There cannot be the least doubt about it…" Before the writer detailed the plight of these poor, "terrified" young men, he first established that the entire community was in a tizzy about the affectionate apparition. The reporter then aired the reactions of the town's women, which were as follows:

> In the opinion of the women of Greenfield, the ghost is by far the worst that has ever made its appearance. There have been, according to ghost-seers, all sorts of undesirable ghosts. Such were the ghosts that threw things at innocent people, and smashed crockery; the ghosts that came and stood by people's beds in the dead of night, without having the decency to knock at the door or to say what they wanted; and the ghosts that rattled chains and thumped on the floor overhead merely in order to make themselves disagreeable. The Greenfield ghost is in local feminine estimation, more wicked than

any of her predecessors—for she is a female ghost. It is her loathsome habit to waylay young men in the midnight streets, to kiss them, and then to vanish. Often she throws herself upon young men who are on their way to visit young ladies, and so terrifies them that they flee to their homes or boarding houses, leaving the unhappy young ladies to watch the front door bell in vain expectation. Conduct such as this is to the last degree revolting to every well brought up young woman, and we can understand why the Greenfield ghost is firmly believed by one-half of Greenfield to belong to the satanic host.

After that lengthy diatribe we could be forgiven for wondering whether paragraph breaks existed in 1881. There's not much question that overreaction and hyperbole certainly did! The article also contains an interesting statement about just exactly how many people in the town had seen the ghost. Their numbers were, well, apparently "numberless." And after that less than helpful quantification, the report gets down to the soul, shall we say, of the issue: the young men, their terror and the "Spectre Given to Kissing."

On the night of the 12th of January, young Mr. Smithers, assistant pastor of a recently developed variety of Baptists, was met by the ghost at 9:30 o'clock. He asserts that she approached him from behind with noiseless steps, threw her arms around him, and kissed him before he could call for help. He instantly broke loose and fled to his home, where he was at once put to bed and a physician summoned, who afterward said that the nervous shock which the patient had sustained might easily have proved fatal. Two nights later, and at about the same hour, Mr. Edward Potter, one of the most respected young men of the town, was kissed in front of Esquire Dewey's house, and left insensible on the pavement. He says that the ghost sprang on him suddenly and kissed him three successive times. As he had never before undergone the operation of being kissed, he suffered acutely, not only because of the outrage to his modesty, but because he feared that his life was in danger. He was since wholly recovered from the shock, but he never goes out at night without tying up his mouth with a large "comforter," and keeping a sharp look out for sudden ghosts. On the night of Feb. 3, Mr. Thomas G. Wilson, whose purity of character and freedom from all knowledge of languages have induced the administration to offer him no less than three foreign consulates, but who preferred to earn the proud distinction of being the only Ohioan who ever refused an office, was waylaid by the ghost, kissed within sight of Mrs. Wilson's windows, and afterward brought home by his neighbours, who found him lying in the snow and uttering incoherent moans. These are but samples of the devastation caused by the Greenfield ghost, and so far as is known there is but one young man in the town who is not in terror for his life. The young man in question is a notorious plumber, and though he has repeatedly met the ghost, she has never once offered to kiss him.

By the last paragraph of the article, the journalist had clearly become indignant—not about the ghost, but about the explanation as to whose ghost she might be. The initial points that he rather angrily makes are, nonetheless, possibly well taken.

> The popular theory is that the ghost was originally a New England school teacher, and that she is now wreaking on mankind her vengeance for their neglect of her during her life. This theory is based principally upon the personal appearance of the ghost, who is described as being very tall, very thin, and wholly unable to cast a shadow when one of her edges is presented to the light. This may all be true, but it by no means proves that the ghost is a New England school teacher. It might with equal force be quoted to prove that she was formerly a Boston poet or an eminent female philosopher. The ghost of a New England woman of any kind would never be guilty of kissing, and even could we imagine her entertaining for a moment the idea of perpetrating such a crime, she would be utterly ignorant of the way in which to perpetrate it.

There's no explanation for why a New England ghost might be haunting a Midwestern town, but the scribe's defense of New England women is interesting!

It seems fitting to close by assuring readers of *Haunted Hearts* that the writer of the article did rely on solid sources in explaining how this shocking and serious situation could best be understood.

...a local minister [whose] intelligence and judgment cannot be called in question, told his hearers that the ghost was a supernatural visitor sent to warn the people of the near approach of the end of the world.

So, now we know that, according to reputable sources, when it comes from the lips of a ghost, a kiss is not just a simple kiss but a somehow world-threatening osculation!

Ghost of a Groom

Eleanor May was 25 years old in 1930 when she took a trip to visit Emily, her sister, in Liverpool. One evening Eleanor and Emily attended a dance at the local church. The pair danced most of the evening away, but by midnight Emily was ready to leave. Eleanor, however, wanted to stay. She had made the acquaintance of an awfully nice man, one Freddie Barclay by name. What was more, this Mr. Barclay really knew how to cut a rug—in other words, he was a fabulous dancer.

For a moment Emily hesitated. Would it be all right to leave her sister alone with the man? It was obvious that he was considerably older than either Emily or Eleanor, but he did seem quite the gentleman and Emily's feet were aching. She was just plain anxious to get home, and so, with a quick wave to her sister and the good-hearted admonition of "Don't be late," Emily was gone.

Less than an hour later, proving that he *was* the gentleman Emily had thought he was, Freddie walked Eleanor home. The two had enjoyed themselves so much at the dance that they agreed to meet again, just a few days hence, at a local pub.

Eleanor looked forward to her date with Freddie and was delighted when she saw him waiting for her at the appointed hour. As it turned out, they had as much fun together that night as they had had at the dance, and so they made another date for the following week. Soon they were meeting regularly—always at the same pub.

Emily had grown suspicious of her sister's new friend and tried to point out to Eleanor that the man had never once mentioned so much as a word about where he lived or anything about his family background. With the best of intentions,

Emily voiced her concerns to Eleanor. Sadly, the remarks led to a vicious spat. The argument ended with the sisters refusing to speak to one another and Eleanor storming away, saying that she was going to accept Freddie's proposal of marriage.

Less than a month later, at a ceremony in the pub where they'd met so often, Eleanor and Freddie became husband and wife.

Shortly after their vows were exchanged, Eleanor was distracted by some well-wishers who had happened upon the wedding. By the time she had said good-bye to the friendly folks, Eleanor realized that she couldn't find Freddie. The worried woman had the bartender check the men's washroom, but the man was not there. Freddie was nowhere to be seen.

For days and days, Eleanor searched for her husband, and with each passing hour the bride's sanity slipped further from her grasp. She didn't eat or sleep or change out of her bridal gown.

Soon Emily heard about Eleanor's plight and, despite their quarrel, ran to her sister's side. Together, the two sisters approached the local constabulary. An aging, grizzled sergeant showed a special interest in Eleanor's strange tale. After hearing her out, the man began to speak in quiet, gentle tones.

The name Freddie Barclay was familiar to him. He recalled an incident more than a decade earlier when there had been gossip about a groom vanishing. An investigation at that time had determined that, on the eve of his wedding, Freddie Barclay had killed himself.

After pausing for a moment to let the sisters absorb the information, the sergeant spoke again. "If you ask me," he said, "Freddie Barclay is a ghost."

Eleanor gave a mirthless laugh. "Believe me, officer," she said, "Freddie was very much alive. Of all the people in the world, I should know that—and I do."

"Well, miss," the constable continued, "I guess you can have it your way, but I do have to tell you that the last girl he left at the altar just a few years back made exactly the same claim. I can even show you the man's grave if you wish. It's in the cemetery just across from the pub where you were married."

Eleanor shook her head in silent reply. At that moment she had no desire to visit a cemetery. Nor did she in the future. As a matter of fact, that particular cemetery was a place she avoided for the rest of her unhappy life. The jilted bride never married—or remarried, whichever would be the correct term—and nothing out of the ordinary ever happened to her again.

Well, maybe there was *one* strange thing. Eleanor never removed the wedding ring that Freddie Barclay had placed on her finger as they exchanged nuptials—yet one morning she awoke to find that it was gone. Like Freddie, the ring had simply vanished. Did she ever wonder whether, somewhere near that cemetery across from the pub, another young woman was preparing to marry a handsome man of about 40 with a mysterious past?

Madison's Mistress

During the late 1800s, Sir Charles Madison was a high-ranking officer in the English Navy. His career meant that, although he lived in England, he frequently visited the eastern seaboard of the United States. It didn't take too many trips away from home before Madison became smitten with an American woman. Her name was Shirley. Now, this relationship wouldn't have been a problem except that Sir Charles' wife, Lady Madison, lived in England. Sadly, this tawdry tale of woe only gets worse.

Charles was apparently as wealthy and conniving as he was unfaithful, for his solution to his love dilemma was to use his money and influence to build a hotel in Baltimore, Maryland. As soon as the structure was ready for business, he "hired" his beloved Shirley as the establishment's live-in manager.

It was no coincidence, of course, that there just happened to be a hidden staircase leading from the owner's suite directly to Shirley's, or that Madison stayed at that hotel whenever he was visiting America. The man's plan worked extremely well while the two women in his life were on opposite sides of the Atlantic Ocean. Unfortunately, Sir Charles' good thing began to come to an end the day that his wife expressed an interest in visiting the New World. The trip was soon arranged.

Madison's lust for his mistress may have clouded his judgment as he booked his wife into the hotel that Shirley managed. Not surprisingly, the man soon became indiscreet with his indiscretion and, after only a few days, Lady Madison discovered her husband in his lover's arms. The angry wife reached for the first weapon at hand—a set of fireplace tongs. She swung the heavy length of brass at the other woman, killing her instantly.

With that act, the body of the "hussy" might have been out of the Madisons' lives, but her spirit never left the hotel. As a matter of fact, that hotel is still in operation, and Shirley's ghost is an accepted feature of the place. Guests see her image on the staircase, in the halls and even in their rooms. They also hear the phantom's footsteps as she walks along in her eternity. Voices and music have been heard coming from Shirley's room—although there was no one, at least no living person, in there at the time.

Pond Phantom

Thomas Lofthouse crouched to dip his pail into the pond near his house. Suddenly, an icy shiver ran up his back. Thomas dropped the pail, jolted upright and whirled around, searching to find what it was that had startled him.

There was nothing out of the ordinary anywhere to be seen.

Even so, Thomas could not shake the feeling that something around him was very wrong. Worse, he was sure that someone was staring at him, watching his every move. Something unnatural was at hand, he was sure. He could sense it in every fiber of his being.

The chore of taking water to his vegetable garden could wait until the next day, the distraught man decided. He turned to leave the pond's edge. As he did, he heard his name being called. The voice, like the whispery rustle of a breeze through the grasses, seemed to come from the opposite side of the small body of shallow water. Nervously, the man scanned the area around him. At first he saw nothing. Then, a heartbeat later, Thomas Lofthouse spotted an image, an image of a young woman. It was Mary, his sister. She was standing just across the water from him.

Confused that Mary, who lived with her husband in the nearby village, would be standing there calling him, Thomas beckoned to her. The young woman's image began to move. It floated across the pond, just above the surface of the water.

Terrified, Thomas fled for home.

When he had recovered sufficiently, the man told his wife what he had seen and heard.

"It was probably just your imagination," the woman offered. "You've been worried about your sister ever since she married William Barwick. I'll tell you what, we have to go to town after lunch anyway, so we'll stop by and pay Mary a visit while we're there. That should ease your mind."

Thomas could only nod.

That afternoon when they arrived at Mary's home, William greeted them. "Mary's not here, I'm afraid," he told them. "She's gone to visit her uncle."

Thomas Lofthouse felt faint when he heard that news from his brother-in-law. He knew then for certain that something very serious had happened to his sister, because Mary detested their uncle and would never have gone to visit him. Thomas and his wife left Barwick's front step and went directly to the town constable. The policeman dispatched his deputy to search the area, and sadly, before the sun had set that evening, Mary's body had been found. She had been strangled and then buried in a shallow grave near the pond where Thomas had seen and heard her image.

It seems that when William Barwick discovered that his bride was pregnant, he no longer wanted anything to do with her and so had killed her. The murderer's plans did not work out too well, though. He was executed—and perhaps forced to face his victim and their unborn child in their eternities.

Heartbeats:
A Collection of Short Stories

Still Searching

It's difficult to find a lighthouse anywhere in the world that doesn't have a ghost story associated with it. And the "light" on St. Martin Island in Lake Michigan is no exception. The spirit of the grieving man who was once the lightkeeper has not found peace—not even centuries after his death.

History tells us that, every morning, the man's beloved children would climb into a small boat to row to a nearby island, where they would attend school. After classes were over for the day, the youngsters would row back to their lighthouse home and the father who loved them dearly. One afternoon, however, a terrible squall blew in. As the worried lighthouse keeper watched, the water became more and more turbulent until the waves seemed alive with a deadly frenzy.

Scanning the horizon for a glimpse of the rowboat that should have been carrying his children safely home to him, he could see nothing but vicious whitecaps swirling about on the normally calm waters. Then, just for an instant, the father was sure that he had finally caught sight of the boat with the children in it. He was even sure that he could hear their plaintive, fearful cries as the enormous waves buffeted them about. But then, as the next swell gave way and the man continued to peer through the spray, there was nothing there. Tragically, the little rowboat that should have ridden atop that next wave was gone from sight, never to appear again. The lighthouse keeper's children had drowned before his eyes.

After the dreadful storm abated, the man searched the shorelines, but the lake had not only claimed the young lives, but it refused to give up their bodies.

Ever since then, sailors have told of seeing a strange green light on the shores of St. Martin Island. They say it is the ghost of the heartbroken lighthouse keeper, searching into eternity for his beloved children.

All the Kings' Men

England's King Charles II was a busy man during his reign (1660–85). In addition to his duties as a monarch, the man had an impressive series of mistresses, including Nell Gwyn, a popular actress of the day. Despite Charles' own philandering ways, he was furious when he learned that Nell was being unfaithful to him. The king's men arrived at her doorstep intent on solving this infidelity problem in a very permanent way. Less than an hour later, Captain John Molineux, Nell's lover, was dead. He had paid the ultimate price for his forbidden love.

The house where Molineux died still stands in London's Soho district. It is said that, even today, more than 300 years after his murder, Molineux's spirit continues to haunt the place. The lovelorn ghost can be heard walking about as well as opening and closing doors. Although he's never harmed anyone, his mere presence has given a few people the scare of their lives!

But what of Nell herself? Sadly, it seems that the king's lover does not rest in peace either. Her ghost haunts Salisbury Hall, the country home north of London where she often entertained her lovers, especially King Charles II. Her pathetic image hovers near the staircase, perhaps waiting in vain to escort the king upstairs to her boudoir.

Love Legend

This ghostly legend has been passed down from generation to generation ever since the original events transpired during the earliest days of the War of 1812 between the United States and Britain.

Marie McIntosh was a beautiful young woman who lived with her parents in Windsor, in what is now Ontario, Canada. Not surprisingly, she was sought after by all the eligible young men in the neighborhood. One man, William Muir by name, loved the fair Marie especially well. When the war broke out, Muir did not hesitate to enlist but, before he went off to battle, he asked Marie if she would marry him. The proposal took the young woman so much by surprise that she wasn't able to give Muir a proper answer immediately.

That night, Marie awakened suddenly. At first she couldn't understand what had disturbed her sleep. She sat up in bed and looked around the darkened room. Then she gasped and shook her head in disbelief as she discerned a figure standing at the end of her bed. It was William Muir! Marie quickly pulled the covers up around her. As she did, Muir's image spoke to her.

"I have died an honorable death," the apparition told the woman he loved, "but my body lies crumpled in the underbrush. Please see that it is found and buried properly."

As Marie nodded in agreement to the entity's request, the image faded from sight.

The next morning, the distraught and grieving young woman told her father about the encounter the night before. The man sent a search party out to scout the woods. They found the soldier's body, just as the ghost had said they would, crumpled in the underbrush. He was buried the next day with appropriate military honors.

Breaking Up Can Be Deadly

The house that some say is the most haunted in the western hemisphere stands at Montego Bay, Jamaica. The Rose Hall Greathouse dates back to the mid-1700s. By 1770 it was owned by a woman named Annie Palmer. Now, Annie was a loving woman, in one sense of the word. She was renowned for having "loved" and then killed as many as a dozen men! In death, she's apparently as restless as she was in life, for her spirit still haunts her former home. Some locals who have generational roots entwining back to those early days refuse to go near that property, for fear of encountering the ghost of the woman who ended her many affairs in a very permanent way.

Better never to have loved than to have loved Annie and be lost forever!

Inn Love

For four centuries, the Inn at Lathones in Scotland has welcomed weary travelers. A stone above the huge fireplace commemorates the marriage of two of the previous innkeepers. Iona Kirk and Ewan Lindsay were married in 1718. Legend has it that when Iona died less than 20 years later, a large crack appeared in that decorative stone.

Ewan's will to live apparently died along with his wife and he succumbed, some say of a broken heart, not long after. It is only her ghost, however, that has returned to haunt the inn the loving couple ran. It's long been presumed that the ghost of the woman haunting the bar area of the inn is that of Iona, who seems content to spend her eternity in the place where she lived and loved.

Ghostly Directions

Author Pauline Saltzman, a veritable pioneer in the field of true ghost story literature, tells an amazing anecdote in her book *The Strange and the Supernatural.* Saltzman writes that Gouverneur Morris of New York State, one of the men responsible for drafting the United States' Constitution, was an early-day American aristocrat. On New Year's Eve, 1816, Morris's ghost returned to his young widow. The spirit showed her where he had hidden valuables that would help to support her financially while she raised their infant son.

The George

An English pub without a ghost would be almost as much of a travesty as an English pub without kegs of good, dark ale. The George, a pub in Robertsbridge, Sussex, is a more-than-respectable establishment in both regards, for it has certainly never run short of ale and it is most definitely haunted.

The ghost may date back to the old days when the building was used as a coach house, because the entity's antics are quite specific and don't seem to relate to the pub itself. It seems that on the George's second floor there is a large room that can be rented out for large gatherings such as weddings. If the phantom is haunted by the thought of the marriage and doesn't predict that the union will be a successful one, the guests will be treated to bumping sounds mysteriously echoing throughout the room.

Although this legend is well-known, there are as yet no records of people calling off their marriage because of these supernatural warnings!

Both Lovers Are Ghosts

In Austria, not far from Vienna, stands a monastery that was once used by nobility as a hunting lodge. That history has left the monastery haunted by the sorrowful ghost of Prince Rudolf, who, along with his beloved young mistress Mary Vetsera, died mysteriously in bed. It has never been clear whether the deaths were a result of a suicide pact or whether they were both murdered. All that is known for certain is that neither of the lovers lived to see the dawn of January 31, 1889.

Over the years, the occasional photograph has shown an apparition roaming the huge, old building. Some say it is the ghost of Prince Rudolf searching for Mary. Others speculate that the image is the ghost of the murderer, whose conscience will not let him rest.

Interestingly, Mary Vetsera's ghost has been seen at the Imperial Palace in Vienna. Her forlorn spirit appears as a white mist, forever making her way to Prince Rudolf's quarters.

Eight Is Enough

In the 1500s, the Château de la Caze was a family's castle home. Today, it is a fine hotel in southeastern France. There is no question as to who the ghosts at the inn are because their pictures still adorn the castle walls. These are the eight daughters of the former owners, the de Mallian family. Although men from near and far came to woo the sisters, no man ever succeeded in winning even one of the girls' hearts, and the sisters all died as lonely, bitter spinsters. Their images have been seen wandering about as though they are looking for someone or something—no doubt the love that, in life, they were never able to find.

Skryne Castle Haunting

The Hill of Tara, in County Meath, Ireland, has been described as the one place on earth that encapsulates the very essence of the Irish, their hearts and souls, their spirit and mystique. On this beautiful, windswept, representative land stands the 900-year-old Skryne Castle, which since the mid-1700s has been home to the pathetic ghost of Lilith Palmerston.

Lilith's parents died when the girl was just a child, and so a family friend, Sir Bromley Casway, took over the responsibility for Lilith's care. The unlikely but happy pair isolated themselves from most of the rest of the world in Casway's home, Skryne Castle. As a result, Lilith grew to an innocent maturity, sheltered and protected from the harshness of the outside world.

Oddly, one of the very few people Sir Bromley associated with was a rough and vile neighbor named Phelim Sellers. It seems that Sellers' wife had died under highly suspicious circumstances only a few years before. Considering Casway's station in life and his responsibility for Lilith, the friendship between these two men seems decidedly strange, but the truth was they *were* friends and Sellers was a frequent guest in the castle.

For as long as she could remember knowing him, Lilith had been uncomfortable when Sellers visited. For reasons she could never quite explain, she was afraid of the man. Soon after the girl reached puberty, this neighbor whom she despised made amorous advances toward Lilith. She told her guardian what had happened and Sir Bromley immediately made arrangements for the two of them to move to Dublin. As a matter of fact, they were ready to leave the very next day.

When Sellers heard about Casway's plan, he flew into a rage. He was determined that, if he could not have Lilith's affections, then no one could. That night, the night that was to be the last one Lilith ever spent in Skryne Castle, Phelim Sellers broke into the girl's castle room. Moments later, Lilith Palmerston lay dead. The man whose "love" she rejected had strangled her.

Not long after he committed the dreadful crime, Sellers was convicted and hanged. That punishment was clearly not enough to allow the girl's soul to rest in peace, for her ghost, still clutching at her throat and wearing the white nightgown she'd had on when Sellers murdered her, has been seen running through the castle corridors. Even when her wronged spirit cannot be seen, the ghost of Lilith Palmerston has been heard shrieking in terror as she eternally relives her terrifying last moments of life on the Hill of Tara.

Cardiff Castle

There are, of course, many different kinds of love. A person's heart may be haunted, or broken, as tragically by the loss of a child as by the loss of a lover. This is certainly the case at the Castell Coch, near Cardiff, Wales. There the ghost of the long-deceased Dame Griffiths still searches for her son, who drowned in a pond on the castle property. It is said that she died from the grief, a grief that has plagued her long into her afterlife.

Love Gone Wrong

Naivete was perhaps the worst quality you could have accused young Rosemary of having. But then, coming of age in the tiny English hamlet of Eridge Green during the 1800s was hardly a circumstance that would have bred sophistication into any girl.

Although she had almost no one to compare him to, Rosemary was convinced that her beau, Glendon, was the most desirable young man in the world. She lived for their stolen moments together in the barn behind the village hall.

She also died for them.

Glendon was certainly not a bad boy. He was no more worldly than Rosemary, and so, just a few months after their relationship had first ignited and she declared she was pregnant, the young man panicked and fled.

Utterly heartbroken and terrified, the girl chose the only option she felt was available to her. Through a veil of tears, Rosemary found a length of cord lying in a corner of the deserted barn. Numbly, with the rope over her shoulder, she climbed to the barn's loft. She knotted one end of the rope securely around a rafter and tied the other end around her own neck. After saying a quick prayer for the soul of her unborn child, she jumped to her death.

When Rosemary did not come home for supper that night, her mother sent the girl's brother off to look for her. Sadly, the boy found his sister, her lifeless body dangling from the rope.

Word of the tragedy raged through the tiny community like wildfire. Once Glendon's family heard, they rushed to find the young man before someone else could tell him of his great loss. But no one could find the lad. By evening, his parents were certain that their son was somehow involved with Rosemary's death. They were also certain that they would likely never see their son again. It seems they were right.

Everyone in the village mourned the young couple and their love that had gone so tragically wrong. It took many, many days for life in the tiny hamlet of Eridge Green to return to normal, but eventually it did. The nights, however, were never the same. The ghostly cries and anguished moans of Rosemary's heartbreak echoed in the air as a constant reminder that two of the town's children, and an unknown third, had been taken away. Rosemary's spirit mourned the loss of Glendon, the loss of her unborn child and the loss of her own life.

Rosemary's life on earth may have been short, but for more than 100 years after her death, the girl's sorrowful phantom laments could still be heard echoing from the barn where she and Glendon created and destroyed life—all in the name of love.

Together Forever

The ruins of the Carlingford Abbey in County Louth, Ireland, are home to the ghost of Henrietta Tradescant, who lived in the 1400s. This female pirate was said to have been utterly devastated when Nevin O'Neill, the man she loved, was lost at sea. Thankfully, the two have apparently been reunited in their afterlives, for their images have been seen walking hand-in-hand along the shore near the crumbled remains of the abbey.

Reluctant Winner

In Bath, England, a pub called the Garrick's Head is said to be haunted by the ghost of a girl who was "won" in a game of cards played in the 1700s. She was so appalled at the thought of having to be with the man who won her that she hanged herself. People, including the pub manager, regularly report becoming aware of her forlorn presence in the place.

Tragic Love

Aaron Burr is one of the most colorful and tragic figures in American history. In 1800, when he was 44 years old, Burr ran for president. When the ballots were counted, it was determined that he and Thomas Jefferson had tied in the number of electoral votes they received. The House of Representatives feared Burr's anti-federalist leanings and broke the tie in Jefferson's favor. Burr became vice president.

Four years later, Burr ran for governor of New York. There again his political efforts were stymied at every turn, this time specifically by the politically powerful Alexander Hamilton. In 1804, frus-
trated and angry that this man who had once been his political ally would thwart his campaign, Aaron Burr challenged Hamilton to an illegal duel. The rest, as they say, is history. Hamilton died. Burr lived. His career, though, along with any hope for a happy or productive life, ended with that fatal shot.

By the time he died in 1836, Burr was a mere shell of the man he had once been. His beloved wife, Theodosia Barstow, had died in 1794. Their daughter, also Theodosia, took

Aaron Burr

over many of her mother's roles in Burr's life. The young woman became her father's companion and hostess. The two grew to be very dependent on one another. Even after young Theodosia's marriage, father and daughter remained close, and the final heartbreak of the man's life came in the form of a shipwreck that took his adored daughter's life.

If his ghost's activities are any indication, it was that last blow that was the hardest for Burr's soul to bear. Although his nattily dressed apparition has been spotted in a Greenwich Village café built on land that Burr once owned, his image has also been seen in Manhattan, near the financial area of Wall Street. The piteously sad phantom is not worried about his investments, though. He's looking out at the waterfront in the futile hope that his much-loved daughter will somehow, in the afterlife, return to his side.

Globe Ghost

In life, Scotland's national poet, Robert Burns, haunted a pub called the Globe Inn. Today, the establishment, located in the city of Dumfries on Scotland's west coast, is a virtual shrine to the poet. Yet no one has ever reported seeing even a glimpse of the small-framed man's spirit since his death in 1796.

The pub was certainly important to the man, though, for it was there that he met and fell in love with a pretty young barmaid, Anna Park by name. Burns immortalized his love for Anna in some of his most famous and poetic lines of love. But the relationship was doomed from the start, for Burns was already a married man with a family. Despite this, Anna became pregnant. She died shortly after giving birth to the poet's illegitimate baby. Burns' wife took the child in and raised it along with her other children.

Even today, it's said that every so often Anna Park's image appears at the Globe Inn. She rarely misses a party, and her presence has also been noted on occasions when the business changes hands. Perhaps she's hoping to catch a glimpse of the spirit of Robbie Burns, should he ever drop in for a wee dram and a visit to his old haunt.

Restless Wraith

Class consciousness, ethnic prejudice and religious bigotry have caused many broken hearts throughout history. In some instances, like the following, those broken hearts have left behind ghost stories.

John Rutledge was born into money. In the early 1800s, in South Carolina, that fact was considerably more important than it might be today. His parents owned a huge plantation that they looked forward to passing on to John—but certainly not if he carried through with his plan to marry the daughter of a lowly merchant, in this case, a local pharmacist. That John's parents could never accept.

What made the matter even worse was that the girl's family did not approve of the marriage, either. They did not want her to marry into a home where she and her parents would not be welcome.

The families' attitudes and John's devotion to his beloved combined to send the young man into a depression—a depression so deep that he never did recover from it. Within the year, he had killed himself.

Sadly, even death did not bring the poor, heartsick soul any peace. His spirit was reported to have roamed his parents' palatial plantation home for years after his death.

Ship of Love

Should you ever be fortunate enough to visit the vibrant seaside city of Brighton on England's south coast, there will be many attractions for you to explore. For centuries, the community has been known as a rendezvous spot for good times, and, even today, nightlife remains an important component of the atmosphere. But there is so much more.

Brighton's humble beginnings as a tiny fishing village changed dramatically in 1750, when Dr. Richard Russell "discovered" the place and touted its seawater as a cure for an amazing assortment of ailments. People, including royalty, began to flock to the shoreside town. That heritage created a legacy of exotic architecture which, in turn, attracted all manner of artists, endowing the city with a rich and fascinating culture that's enjoyed by residents and visitors all year round. For those of us with a particular interest in ghostly romance, though, the best time to see Brighton is on May 17 each year—for that is when the heartsick spirit of Lady Edona walks the earth.

The noblewoman, from medieval times, was in love with the dashing and well-connected Manfred de Warrenne. Manfred, it seemed, was something of a romantic. Before he would marry his beloved Lady Edona, he was determined to make a pilgrimage to Jerusalem. Perhaps honored by his evident devotion to her, Lady Edona waited patiently for him at Lewes Castle near Brighton.

On May 17, when word was received that her beloved's ship had been spotted off the coast, Lady Edona rushed to the seashore to welcome Manfred home from his long and arduous voyage. Tragically, as his ship approached, it struck a submerged rock and sank. All but one soul, not Manfred, perished. The suitor and the noblewoman would never be reunited, at least not in this life.

We could hope that their spirits at least found each other. Not only did Manfred die that day, but so also did Lady Edona—she died of shock at having witnessed the ship sinking and taking her lover's life with it.

Alas, they may not yet be reunited in the afterlife. Ever since that fateful day, on May 17 each year, it is said that the phantom image of Manfred de Warrenne's ship can be seen just where it sank off the coast of Brighton. And Lady Edona stands on the shore, still awaiting in vain his safe return.

Barnsley's Tragic Folly

Godfrey Barnsley was not much more than a boy in 1823 when he left his home in England and made his way to America. The ambitious young immigrant had little education and less money, but he was hardworking and determined to make a success of himself. Within five years Barnsley more than realized his goal. He made a veritable fortune in land development and attained an enviable position in the state of Georgia's social hierarchy. As a matter of fact, he cut such a romantic figure that it is said author Margaret Mitchell in part modeled Rhett Butler, her hero in the novel *Gone With the Wind*, after Barnsley.

On Christmas Eve of 1828, the wealthy and dashing Barnsley married Julia Scarborough, daughter of a prominent local family. Barnsley's future was assured. His business ventures continued to be profitable, he and his wife were deeply in love and soon they were the parents of many much-adored children. Misfortune, it seemed, would never touch this family.

Even when Barnsley noticed that his beloved Julia was no longer in robust health, the devoted husband was sure he could solve the problem by moving his family away from the sweltering heat of the lowlands to a higher elevation in the northwestern part of the state. And he knew just the spot he would move them to. You see, while traveling on business, the man had seen what he considered the most beautiful area imaginable. He knew for certain that the land was vacant because the Cherokee had just been driven away from the area. Barnsley acted immediately. He bought over 4000 acres and soon had moved his family to a temporary residence there.

Godfrey and Julia set about planning to build a mansion that would be surrounded by lavish gardens filled with exotic foliage. There was a lot of work ahead of them, they knew, but the cooler climate would be so much better for Julia's health, and their new home would be nothing short of splendid.

During his exploration of the enormous property he had purchased, Godfrey Barnsley had been surprised to find one remaining Cherokee still living where his people had resided for generations. It did not take long for the two men to shape a deal, and soon the native man was working for the newcomer. The arrangement worked well for both parties. Barnsley provided the old-timer with food and shelter, while the native man was able to familiarize the new owner with the area.

All went well until the Barnsleys began to plan exactly where, on this enormous tract of land, they would place their future home. Godfrey found an oddly shaped hill on the property. It appealed to him as a location for the house and he began to prepare an area for the construction to follow. In order to make the building process easier, a portion of the hill would have to be cut off. No sooner had work been started than the old Cherokee man raced to Barnsley's side, urging him not to dig at that particular spot. The mound, he explained, was sacred to the Cherokee Nation and the spirits of their native forefathers would never forgive anyone who desecrated it.

Barnsley, of course, was a successful white businessman who had experienced nothing but good luck since moving to America and had no appreciation of the native North American culture. He ignored the man's desperate warning and proceeded with his plans. The wealthy man never saw the elderly native again. It's likely, though, that Barnsley thought of that Cherokee and his dire warning many, many times over the years to come.

Barnsley's much-loved wife became very ill after her last pregnancy and, despite all the money and resources he invested in medical care, first his infant son and then his beloved wife died in 1844. The man was devastated by his loss. He no longer had any interest in completing the home he had intended to build for the family, but instead devoted himself solely to his businesses.

In his grief, Barnsley became interested in psychic phenomena and began attending séances, no doubt hoping for some kind of contact with his deceased wife. Eventually, while he was on the section of land that he and Julia had once happily planned as the garden of their home, the woman's ghost visited him. She urged her husband to finish the home and the garden, just as they had designed them. Her ghostly words were, apparently, all the grieving man needed. Before too long a three-story, 24-room, red-brick villa stood on the cutaway land that the Cherokee had pleaded should be left as it was.

Soon, the home was the envy of anyone who knew of it. And no wonder—the place was truly spectacular. It even had an extremely inventive system of copper tanks to supply both hot and cold running water to the house, a luxury few had thought possible in that era.

But the house, it seemed, was not to become the dream family home that Godfrey and Julia had planned. In 1850, their eldest daughter broke her father's heart by marrying and moving to England. Eight years later, their second daughter died. If Barnsley was not suspicious by that time that he was living with the ancient anger the Cherokee man had warned him about, he surely must have become so when the next round of bad luck hit. His oldest son was killed by pirates while on an expedition in the Orient. The son had been searching for exotic plants to complement the garden surrounding his father's Georgia mansion.

By the time the Civil War broke out, Barnsley had still not completed his palatial home, but had toured Europe choosing furnishings for the place. Troops invaded the oddly incomplete yet exotically partly furnished home. Soldiers trashed the interior of the house, but the shell of the building remained standing. At the war's end, the Barnsley family home was a broken travesty of its former self. Worse, the two sons who remained fled to South America to escape the outcome of the war. Godfrey Barnsley moved to New Orleans, where he died in 1873.

The ghostly encounters within the Barnsley family did not stop with Julia's spirit encouraging her husband to finish their dream home. Even one of Julia's granddaughters reported frequently seeing her grandmother's apparition on the property. The younger woman also maintained that, on the day that one of Godfrey and Julia's sons died in South America, his image returned to the old family home.

In 1906, a tornado nearly blew the crumbling old family mansion to bits, but even then the curse was not satisfied. Members of the third and fourth generations of the family who attempted to live on the jinxed land could not escape terrible misfortune. Godfrey and Julia's granddaughter Adelaide lived on the property with her two young sons, Preston and Harry. Preston became a successful professional boxer, and for a while he spent much of his income on attempting to maintain the old homestead. After a few years, however, he fell victim to that frequent occupational hazard of the prizefighter—a brain injury. He was deemed to be psychologically unfit and was incarcerated in a mental asylum. Despite being in a locked and guarded facility, Preston escaped and, in a fit of delusional fury, sure his brother was trying to steal his rightful portion of the family home, murdered his own brother. Adelaide held her dying son as he breathed his last breath in the home built so long ago on desecrated land.

Adelaide died in 1942. The crumbling mansion and all its remaining furnishings and decorations were sold at auction. Then, for a time, the land surrounding the old Barnsley mansion was farmed.

In 1989, Prince Fugger of Germany bought the estate. One of his first endeavors on the property was to have two chiefs of the Cherokee Nation remove the curse and bless his future plans for the land. That demonstration of respect and acknowledgment of those whose land it had originally been was obviously much more effective than Godfrey Barnsley's disregard of the ancients more than a century before. The prince's business, an exclusive resort and golf course, has been a success.

Could all the tragedies that befell the loving, but impulsive, Godfrey Barnsley and his descendants have been avoided, if only he had heeded the native man's warning and chosen a location for his house just a few yards away from the cursed spot?

More's the pity that Julia couldn't have warned Barnsley not to proceed with his folly. Perhaps, like Godfrey, Julia's spirit lacked a full appreciation for native North American culture. Passage to an afterlife apparently doesn't necessarily guarantee enlightenment.

Japanese Jenny

When internationally renowned psychic Lyn Inglis was asked to visit a particular house in a small western Canadian city, she was not too surprised. After all, for years her psychic gifts have taken her on many complex and intriguing journeys. Even police forces from various cities occasionally call on Ms. Inglis's talents when their usual investigative procedures leave them stumped. In this case, however, it was a home-owner, a prominent member of his community, who had contacted Lyn. The two first met when Lyn was conducting a meditation seminar.

"I had asked everyone who attended to bring some-thing—just some small thing—of theirs with them for the meditation. Dave chose to bring a pot of colored stones," Lyn remembered.

Dave spilled the stones out for Lyn to examine. "I imme-diately picked out one particular stone and set it aside. I told him, 'This one doesn't belong with the others.' He acknowl-edged that I was correct, that he had placed that one stone in as a decoy to see if I could spot it."

So, having apparently passed the test that Dave had devised for her, Lyn proceeded with the man's meditative reading. As usually happens under these circumstances, the two came to know one another as the session progressed. One of the comments Dave made indicated that he felt there was something out of the ordinary about the home he had recently bought and moved into.

"It's a lovely big house," Lyn explained. "It was built in the 1940s, but in the style of a heritage home. He said that an area extending from the basement straight up to the third floor made everyone feel uncomfortable and no one would go into those parts of the house. Dave had also noticed that, since moving into the place, and despite his best efforts, nothing good seemed to manifest in his life. There just seemed to be a negative, disruptive energy in the place."

He had come to believe that the house was haunted.

At Dave's request, Lyn visited his home. She quickly realized that the soul haunting the man's house had nothing at all to do with the residence itself. Using her natural gift of telepathy, which Lyn has tested and perfected throughout her entire lifetime, impressions, words and pictures began to form in her mind. Soon, she knew that the presence had been in that spot—the area of Dave's house in which no one felt comfortable—for a century. The spirit apparently had no idea she was dead.

Once Lyn had established those basic facts, other information came to her. The ghost was the spirit of a young woman who had been murdered there nearly 100 years earlier. The girl's story, fleshed out by later research, is a tragedy from beginning to end.

"Her name was Jenny," Lyn began.

In about the early 1900s, the girl had been lured from Japan to Vancouver with the promise of marriage to an eligible man. Tragically, that

Psychic Lyn Inglis helped Jenny's brokenhearted ghost find freedom.

pledge was utterly false, merely a ruse to entice girls to North America's frontier towns. The young woman's ship had no sooner docked than the terrified girl was given the name "Japanese Jenny" and forced into a life of the most demeaning form of servitude—prostitution.

After a few miserable months working in the horrors of the port city's sex trade, Jenny was shipped inland. Here she met a young man who truly loved her. Soon, the pair made plans to run away together.

Unfortunately, word of their plans somehow leaked out, and the owner of the brothel where Jenny worked was furious. The next day, her crumpled body was found lying on a small rise, in a stand of trees, down by the river. There was, of course, an investigation. Jenny's pimp was charged and incarcerated.

Lyn continued, "Some years later, though, more evidence apparently came to light which proved that the brothel owner had actually been innocent of Jenny's murder and so he was released. Another man, the one who had really been the murderer, was arrested, tried and punished for the crime."

After that, for the living, life went on. By the 1940s, the trees that had stood as silent sentinels over Jenny's lifeless body all those years ago were felled to make room for a big, new house—the very house that, many years later, Dave would buy. Of course, he had no way of knowing that it had been built on a place where a murder had been committed.

"Jenny wasn't a bad spirit in any way," Lyn explained. "Her great sadness created negative energy that was disruptive."

As Lyn worked her way through the process of clearing Dave's house, she had to explain to the murdered young woman that she was no longer alive and that 100 years had passed since she had been.

"There's no time in the other world," Lyn explained. "In order to help her I also had to call on the energy of the man she'd intended to marry. He had left town after Jenny's murder and had lived the rest of his life in Alberta."

Of course, he too had been dead for many years by then.

"Eventually, her soul passed over, but it took me an entire weekend to do it," Lyn acknowledged.

But for all of those involved, from this world and the next, the effort was more than worthwhile. With her compassionate and loving nature, as well as her extraordinary psychic abilities, Lyn was finally able to free the tragic soul once known as "Japanese Jenny" from her earthly tethers, allowing her to move along to her eternal rest and perhaps reunite with the spirit of the man who once loved her. And Dave's house has been a warm and positive home ever since.

The story didn't end there—not quite. The entire psychic procedure had apparently made Dave intensely curious and so he set about scanning his community's archival news files. He found documents reporting on the murder of a young Japanese prostitute whose body was found in a grove of trees near the river. All the information was there. Every word attested to the accuracy of Lyn's clairsentience!

Supernatural Cupid

In the fall of 1973, Erika Braune was barely able to maintain the obligations that supported her life. She was reeling from the breakup of her marriage. As best as she was able, the woman managed to continue her job as a yoga teacher in West Seneca, New York, but that was about all. All other commitments had been completely wiped off her calendar. For this reason, when she received an invitation to attend a regular meeting of the psychic forum she belonged to, Erika hesitated. She relented and agreed to join the others only when she was told that, without her, there would be no one at the gathering who had any abilities as a medium.

Although the distressed and distracted woman hoped that the demands on her psychic abilities would not be too onerous that evening, one of the attendees, a man named Gerald Welsted, did ask that she help him contact a favorite relative, his deceased Aunt Gertie. Much to Erika's surprise, she was able to make the connection beyond with little effort. It almost seemed as though the spirit of Gerald's Aunt Gertie had been waiting to be contacted. The message the spirit had for the living was also surprising.

"Erika, marry Gerald," the entity instructed.

At first, no one in the group, especially Erika and Gerald, knew what to make of the entity's directions. It's not that there was anything ambiguous about the statement. As a matter of fact, it was about as straightforward as anything could possibly be. Yet the two people barely knew each other, and besides, Erika was still grieving her recently failed relationship.

The pair tried to forget the content of the message, but this strange, shared experience served to get them talking more than they otherwise would have. Soon, those chats were taking the form of dates. Happily, the more Gerald and Erika came to know one another, the more they enjoyed each other's company. When they married only weeks later, Gerald's Aunt Gertie, their supernatural cupid, must have been a happy soul!

A Happy Ending

Barbara McDonald was as happy in 1970 as she had ever been in her life. She had a good job in Washington, D.C., she enjoyed the company of wonderful friends and she was engaged to be married. Or so she thought.

One day in June 1971, she found out that her best friend and her fiancé had eloped the previous night. Barbara was overwrought with grief and anger. For days she stayed in her apartment crying her eyes out. No one could console her.

Then, one day, as she lay sobbing on her bed, Barbara suddenly felt strangely calm and consoled. Oddly, she felt as though there was a loving presence in the room with her. All her ill feelings began to disappear. Moments later, she lifted her head up from the pillow and opened her eyes. A misty image stood before her. The apparition moved toward Barbara. It sat down beside her and held the brokenhearted young woman in a loving embrace as she cried and cried until her tears were spent. Only then did Barbara fully realize that she was being comforted by an ethereal being. With this startling realization, Barbara screamed hysterically.

Her neighbor in the apartment upstairs heard the terrified woman's screams and ran to her door. He yelled at her to open up or he would call the police. Barbara staggered to the front hall and let the young man into her apartment before falling to the floor in a faint. The concerned young man carried the unconscious woman to the sofa and stayed with her until she regained consciousness.

When she insisted that there was no one he could call to come and be with her for the rest of the day, the Good Samaritan neighbor stayed there himself. That night, Barbara was beginning to feel better, and so the two went out to a movie together. It was their first date. Within a year, Barbara McDonald had married her neighbor, the young man brought into her life thanks to the ministrations of a kindly spirit.

Who Calls?

When European explorers made their way onto the prairie lands of North America in the late 18th and early 19th centuries, they were struck by the haunting beauty of a particular valley in what is now the Canadian province of Saskatchewan. Daniel Harmon was then a fur trader with the North West Company. He was told by a native leader, whose ancestors had lived in the bountiful valley for generations, why the native people called the place "Kahtapwao" or "Catabuysepu," meaning "What is calling?"

It seems that a handsome young Cree man was very much in love. As he made his way back to his summer home camp after having been away on a solitary voyage, he paddled with all his strength. Every fiber of the man's being wanted to get back to the comely maiden who was waiting impatiently for him to return so that the two could wed. The young man's intense emotions drove him to paddle hour after hour, day after day, barely stopping for food and rarely stopping to rest. Finally one evening he realized with joy and relief that he was just a day away from resting his eyes on his beautiful bride-to-be. Pausing for a moment, he let that blissful thought wash over him.

Strangely enough, in the utter silence and solitude, the man thought he could hear a human voice. Straining his senses, he could see nothing except the beautiful waterway that had been his path as it coursed through the lush wide valley.

But there it was again! That voice! It was clear enough this time that he knew someone was calling his name.

"Who calls?" he shouted from his canoe, but only the valley walls answered him with mocking echoes: *Who calls? Who calls? Who calls? Who calls?*

Qu'Appelle River, Saskatchewan

Frightened by the eerie echo reverberating through the darkening shadows of evening, and afraid that somehow the discomforting encounter was an omen of tragedy, the man began to paddle at a feverish pace. He would get home soon, see his beloved and know that all was well.

Alas, as he propelled his canoe faster and faster toward home, the man's assurances to himself proved to be in vain. As he approached the place where his people were camped, he could see fires lit along the shoreline. Those were death fires, he knew. He also knew that the maiden he loved with all his heart had passed from this life into the next.

As he beached his canoe, elders hurried to take the man to see the body of his beloved lying in repose. The brave was overcome by anguish. Hoping to console him, his people assured the heartbroken young man that the girl had called to him with her dying breath.

"She called for you twice last night," they told him.

"When?" he wailed.

"When the shadows of evening began to darken," they answered.

At least then the Cree brave knew that not only had the fair maiden loved him to the very end, but that *she* had been the one who called out to him—and that their great love for one another had somehow allowed him to hear her cries.

Sadly, even after all these years, it's clear that the heartbroken man's spirit is still not at rest. It is said that you can still hear the echoes of the distraught soul calling out his plaintive queries to the voice he was sure he heard on that fateful evening.

Over the years, the Cree word "Kahtapwao" ("What is calling?") has become the French phrase "Qu'Appelle," meaning "Who calls?" A version of the original word has been retained in the name of Katepwa Point Provincial Park, a recreation area in the vicinity, and so honors the roots of this romantic legend. The essence of the legend is also captured in the name of Echo Valley Provincial Park. Interestingly, the Echo Valley Conference Centre on the shore of Echo Lake is also haunted. That chilling story, told in detail by author Jo-Anne Christensen in her book *Ghost Stories of Saskatchewan*, is far from a romantic tale and not, therefore, suitable for retelling in this volume.

The Swamp

The wetlands of Virginia are also home to a love legend. Lake Drummond, near Norfolk, Virginia, is said to be the haunted setting of a story so romantic that poems have been written about it. Thomas Moore penned a ballad called "The Lake of the Dismal Swamp"; it apparently attracted the attention of the darkly poetic Edgar Allan Poe, and he too described the dramatic location in verse.

The story of this haunting begins many, many years ago, when the area was known by a name that would mortify any modern tourism marketer—the Lake of the Dismal Swamp.

One of the families that had settled near the morass included a fair maiden. The lass fell in love with a handsome young man who lived nearby. As the happiest of good luck would have it, the lad returned the lass's affections. Tragically, though, their happiness was not long lived, for the girl succumbed to a fatal disease. Her body was laid to rest near the swamp.

The loss of his beloved was more than the smitten man could bear. For days after her death, he went without food or sleep. Eventually, even though he began to recover physically, he was never stable mentally again. It seems that he was sure his bride-to-be was not really dead, but that she had been hidden away from him somewhere in the swampy terrain. One day, apparently determined to find his beloved, the frenzied man set out into the bog. Of course, the others from the neighborhood knew that the young woman was dead and the young man was insane, so they set out to find the lad before he died, too—of starvation or exposure.

But the man's determination urged him on into the marshlands and, for a time, he eluded the searchers. All the while, his grip on sanity weakened until he was sure that he could hear his love beckoning to him from the swamp. Rushing to get to her, the man hastily constructed a raft and floated to the center of the water. When his would-be rescuers reached the shore near him, they shouted out instructions to steer the raft toward them. But he wouldn't, of course, because in his tormented mind, the love of his life was near at hand and very much in need of him.

"I see her standing in the light," he told those assembled on the shore. As they watched helplessly and in horror, the poor distraught lover's raft broke apart. The brokenhearted man's body was never found. His apparition, however, was seen for many years, always floating just above the Lake of the Dismal Swamp.

Haunted to Death

This story was reported in both the New York Star *and the* Globe and Mail *in July 1886, and all quotations are from those articles.*

All the members of the Methodist congregation in Bound Brook, New Jersey, felt bad for one of their fellow parishioners. Hebron and his wife, Eva, had been faithful members of the church and had seemed devoted to one another. No wonder the man had been so completely devastated by Eva's premature and unexpected passing that spring. At her funeral, Hebron had confided that, just before his beloved had breathed her last, she had made him promise "that he would never marry again."

You can appreciate the church members' shock and dismay, then, upon learning that Hebron "soon forgot his promise…his wife had been in her grave scarcely six weeks when he sought to soothe his sorrows by wedding Mary Chandler, a buxom widow of some 40 years." To make matters worse, this new wife "was a Roman Catholic, and Hebron immediately renounced his connection with the Methodist Church and embraced Catholicism."

Now, there were those in the community who, from that moment on, simply chose to ignore Hebron's very existence. There were others, though, who continued to visit with their old and once-respected friend, when an appropriate occasion arose. And it was those folks who began to exchange concerned comments. Hebron "acted queerly," one said. "He seemed ill at ease," another assessed. A third went so far as to hypothesize that his friend "had the appearance of a man haunted with some secret trouble." Those speculations, as it turned out, were close to being deadly accurate, for Hebron "said himself that he was troubled with insomnia."

And that insomnia was exactly the reason Hebron was awake in the middle of the night when the Methodist Church, the place of worship he and Eva had once been proud to call their spiritual home, burned to the ground. Hebron and his new wife mingled with the crowd that had gathered to helplessly look on as the flames destroyed the building. "Suddenly, while watching the flames, [Hebron] started back with an exclamation of horror…he appeared as though held by some strange fascination. Then, he shrank back, placed his hands before his eyes, as though to shut out some horrible vision, all the while trembling in every limb."

Soon Hebron's behavior had become so odd that it was clear something was very wrong. One by one, those standing around him lost interest in the fire and began to stare at the man, all the while backing away from him. The crowd watched with shocked fascination as Hebron screamed out in terror. In the moments before his dreadful fright rendered him senseless, he cried out that the ghost of Eva, his dead wife, had manifested in the flames. Worse, "she brought an army of ghastly creatures…ten thousand devils" with her. The supernatural beings "jeered and jibed at him," intent on ending his life. Moments later, "he fell to the ground in a dead faint."

The local doctor, who had been awakened by the noise of the crowd gathered to gawk at the fire, rushed to Hebron's assistance, passing smelling salts under the unconscious man's nostrils. Moments later, barely revived, Hebron was heard to utter a single phrase.

"I am doomed," he said, before passing out once more.

A group of men carried Hebron back to his home, where they laid him on the bed to rest. But, for his tormented soul, rest was now a thing of the past.

"His dreams were hideous, and his wakeful moments frightful. One morning he came to some of his friends with a countenance more ghastly than ever, and told them of a dream he had during the night. He said he thought the skeleton of his first wife lay beside him, and when in terror he sprang from the bed, the specter followed him. At length it pinned him to the wall with one of its long, ghastly fingers, and he felt his life blood ooze from his pierced heart and drop to the floor."

But the haunted man's troubles were not over. "The specter licked up his flowing blood screaming 'So I stop the vitality of my false husband.'"

The description of this bizarre and horrid encounter "convinced Hebron's friends that he was insane, and they took steps to place him in the asylum."

Those well-meaning folks never had to carry out their plan, though, for the next day "he was found dead in his bed." It was later determined that "he had died from fright."

And that is the end of the story as history has left it to us—roughly 120 years of history, for the events related above occurred during July 1886! Such a story, despite its details, does create an absolute myriad of questions in a reader's mind, doesn't it? For instance, were Hebron and Eva reunited in the great beyond? Did Eva forgive her weak-willed husband his trespasses? Were they able to make amends and spend their deaths happily ever after? And what of Mary Chandler, Hebron's "buxom" and "Catholic" second wife? Perhaps she was just relieved to be free of Hebron's haunted heart.

The Birthplace

Telling ghost stories around a campfire is a long and proud Girl Scout tradition. How fitting, then, that America's Girl Scouts have their very own, well-accepted and well-documented haunted-house story.

The mansion at 10 East Oglethorpe in Savannah, Georgia, was built in 1818 for James Moore Wayne, then mayor of the southern city. Sarah and William Gordon bought the elegant Regency townhouse from Mayor Wayne in 1831, and the stately residence remained in the Gordon family's possession for the next four generations.

On Halloween Day in 1860, Juliette Magill Kinzie (Gordon) Low, Sarah and William's granddaughter, was born in the house. Juliette, or "Daisy" as she was fondly known, grew up to become a remarkable woman despite her struggles with deafness, cancer and an unhappy marriage.

In 1912, a year after meeting with Sir Robert Baden-Powell, the founder of the Scouting movement, Daisy started the American Girl Scouts. A mere 18 girls were the first to sign up on March 12 of that first year. By the time Daisy died in 1927, membership in Girl Scouts had grown to an amazing 168,000 active members! From then on, for girls all over the United States, the rest is, of course, history.

Happily, that history still includes the Gordon family home, now often referred to as "the Birthplace" of the Girl Scout founder. The house, a National Historic Landmark, has been owned by the Girl Scouts of the USA since 1953. The Birthplace is a popular destination for visitors to Savannah, and anyone interested in Girl Scouts, in American social and

The beautiful mansion of American Girl Scout founder, Juliette Gordon Low.

women's history, or in a marvelously romantic ghost story will enjoy a stop there.

Staff at the Birthplace acknowledge that, thanks to Daisy's foresight, the poignant legend of love has been told and enjoyed many times. Halloween is an especially busy time at the Birthplace, not only because of the ghost story but also, of course, because the date is the anniversary of Daisy's birth.

The romantic tale involves Daisy's parents and takes place at the time of the death of her mother, Nellie, in 1917. The dying woman had been a widow for five years following the death of her beloved husband, William Washington Gordon II, or Willie, as he was affectionately known.

Mary Stuart Gordon Platt, Daisy's niece, penned the following letter in which she described the ghostly visitation:

> While Daisy and her sisters and brothers were gathered around their mother's bed in the 2nd floor front bedroom bidding her last farewell, Margaret, the wife of Daisy's younger brother George Arthur, waited in an adjoining room for Nellie's death to come. She remembered a time similar to this one several years before when her husband's father breathed his last and how distraught his wife and children had been. This family, into which Margaret had married and which Daisy was an adored member, was an exceptionally devoted one.
>
> Arthur's wife was comforted by the hope that the dying woman in the next room would soon be with her husband whom she had missed so much. What a magnificent old gentleman he had been. How admiring and a little frightened she had been of General Gordon when she first knew him. She would never forget his dignity or the warmth of feeling that gradually developed between them. He had been quieter than the rest of the family but no less loving with a special fondness for animals that his daughter Daisy inherited from him. Margaret smiled to herself as she thought about the dear old man when suddenly she felt another presence in the room with her. On the threshold separating it from the death chamber stood a familiar figure. His hand was turning the knob of the door to close it behind him. Her father-in-law, wearing his favorite suit of light grey, did not see

Margaret at first. His usually serious face was transformed by a grain of gladness when he caught sight of the startled woman. With dawning recognition in his expressive eyes, he passed the way to the hall door. "Come on My Dear," his voice rang out with its old abruptness, then he was gone.

Margaret was white and rigid when her husband joined her a moment later. Thru the barrier of his new sorrow, Arthur duly perceived his wife's agitation. "Your father," Margaret breathed thru stiffened lips—"Yes," he choked without comprehending. "I wish I could believe Mother was with him now—by his side where she so much wanted to be."

"He just came out of her room," Margaret whispered. "I saw him. He spoke to me."

"You are imagining—Dearest—" he drew his hand wearily across his brimming eyes. "Come we must go now, it's over," his voice broke but she didn't hear it—

"Arthur, you don't understand. I've seen your father alive and well."

"Nonsense!" He spoke sharply now. The pain of his loss was becoming unbearable. "We must leave before the others find you in this upset condition. They've been thru enough already."

"I'm sorry Arthur," she tried to steady her taut nerves. Her arms went round him attempting to hold some of the burden of his sorrow. Together they went into the hall and down the great winding staircase. At the foot stood a withered black servant who had been with the family for generations. His head

Nellie and Willie, pictured here, loved each other eternally.

was bent—he raised his eyes to Margaret and Arthur. Holding out a trembling hand he muttered, "Shake this, Mr. Arthur. The General, he just clasped this old hand of mine. He came down these stairs just as plain as you and Miss Margaret." Arthur's stricken face blanched. "What?" he demanded loudly for Cicero was very deaf. "The General said to me, 'Well, Cicero, I have been able to come get Miss Nellie. I am here a while longer.' Then, let's see, he said something instead of goodbye." "Au revoir" Margaret suggested gently. "That's it," the old man exclaimed gratefully. Then he shook my hand hard the way he always used to and gave his salute and he stepped out in his grey suit, same as when the buggy was waiting for him there."

"Miss Margaret also saw him, Cicero," Arthur told the old man gravely as his expression softened.

"O, I'm glad of that. The General always was so proud of your Mrs. He looked well and happy now Mr. Arthur. Happier than I have ever seen him. I'm not going to say anything about this to anybody, but I reckon you'd like to know. The General came to fetch his Mrs. Himself."

Arthur held the feeble hand fervently in his own. "Thank you, Cicero. Yes, I'm comforted to know. Sometimes one comes so close to things one can't see them fully or clearly. May the Lord bless you Cicero, now and always."

"I think we should share what you and Cicero saw and heard this day with the rest of the family," Arthur told his wife on their way home. "They would want to know."

When Daisy heard she said, "I'll always cherish the memory of Mama and Papa and the precious old house where we've all been so happy together. We must let future generations know what Margaret and Cicero told us."

The Gordons' wish that the details of this amazing event be handed down to "future generations" has clearly been respected. Family members still tell the story and have added a further enchanting piece to the paranormal puzzle—a description of what had occurred in "the death chamber" just before both Margaret and Cicero witnessed General Gordon's apparition.

Right before Nellie died, she sat up in bed, stretched out her arms, smiled like a bride, lay back down and slipped peacefully away. Willie, who had died five years before, was seen in an adjoining hallway, looking lovingly into the room where the children were sitting with their mother. Some also say that at that point there was the scent of orange blossoms often used in bridal veils and bridal arrangements in Victorian weddings. Just after Nellie's death, the family butler saw Mr. Gordon come down the stairs and walk out the front door. The butler remarked that Willie looked young, handsome and very happy and that he believed Mr. Gordon had come to get Miss Nellie at last.

It is difficult to imagine a more romantic ghost story—or, for that matter, a more fitting venue for such a tale. The fact that this lovely legend has been passed down through the years is one more reason to be grateful for the sensitivity and foresight of Juliette Gordon Low—"Daisy," founder of the Girl Scouts—and her family.

The Lyttleton Stories

Strange as it may seem, there are two apparently uncon-
nected and markedly different ghostly love stories involving
people with the rather unusual surname of Lyttleton.

Lord Lyttleton was, in a word, a cad. Worse, he was a cad
with an expensive gambling habit. Happily, in late November
of 1779 (on a Thursday, for those interested in such details),
Lyttleton's unconscionable ways did eventually catch up with
him—but not before he had destroyed the life of at least one
other person, a Mrs. Dawson by name.

This particular ghostly love story began when the hateful
Lord Lyttleton set out to seduce the newly married Mrs.
Dawson. He was not a bit interested in the woman for her
good looks or charming ways. No, Lyttleton was merely after
the bridal dowry she'd brought to her marriage. You see, he
owed money to more people than he could count, and those
lenders were beginning to lose patience with his lack of anything approaching a regular repayment schedule. Now, Lord
Lyttleton was good at his ruses; that was undeniable. He was
strikingly handsome and, in this case at least, highly moti-
vated. In the wretched gambler's thieving mind, all he
needed to do was woo Mrs. Dawson's goods away from her
and sell them to clear away his backlog of debt.

Sadly, the naive woman fell for the bounder's lies. She was
convinced that the dashing man was going to sweep her away
from the dull life she'd married into, and that together they
would enjoy lives of glamour and adventure. And so, within
weeks, she had happily given him all her worldly possessions.
Only then did she discover that her appeal for Lyttleton had
diminished as rapidly as her wealth. What Lord Lyttleton did

not count on was the fact that the impoverished Mrs. Dawson had more conscience than he himself had nerve. When the pathetic soul realized that she had been played for a fool, she took her own life.

Now, if this weren't a ghost story, one might think that Lord Lyttleton escaped unpunished, but that was not to be. Mrs. Dawson's ghost began haunting him relentlessly. The woman's apparition was even seen by such notable men of that era as Sir Walter Scott, Dr. Samuel Johnson and author James Boswell. The wronged spirit knew exactly how to best punish her victim. She often came to him in the night, disturbing his sleep. Once she had awakened Lyttleton by manifesting beside his bed, she would terrorize him by whispering threats on his life in her raspy phantom voice.

Hoping that surrounding himself with a crowd would help distract him from the torturous haunting he had brought upon himself, and desperate for a good night's sleep, Lord Lyttleton arranged to host a large party at his London home. As the guests arrived he proclaimed that his hospitality, food and beverages were theirs to enjoy for as long as they wished. With that welcome, the exhausted man took to his bed, hoping that he would sleep undisturbed while the commotion from the party kept the ghost away.

Lord Lyttleton's plan, however, apparently did not work, for the next morning the raucous party was interrupted by the screams of the evil man's servant. He had found his master dead in his bed. The doctor who examined the corpse declared that the man had died of unnatural causes. In the end it seemed Mrs. Dawson had wrought her revenge.

Some 70 years later, in another part of England, a Baron Lyttleton and his wife celebrated a joyous occasion—the birth of their daughter, Mary. The child grew into an attractive and charming young woman. In 1871, when she was barely out of her teens, Mary Lyttleton met British politician Arthur James Balfour, and the two became virtually inseparable. They shared many interests, especially a love of music. If Balfour had been a more forthcoming man in matters of the heart, they would likely have become engaged before the year was out. As it was, the couple's stilted, formal Victorian-style relationship continued, unchanged, for years.

Then tragedy struck. The beautiful young Mary Lyttleton contracted typhoid fever and died before her 25th birthday. Balfour was devastated. Just hours before the casket containing the love of his life was lowered into the ground, he pledged his troth to her by finally placing a ring on her finger, and, according to all accounts, remained faithful to her for the rest of his life.

After a period of deep grieving, Balfour began to pursue his political career once again. Along the way, the Spiritualism movement that had begun sweeping the British Isles and North America also caught his attention. He began attending séances, hoping to regain at least a bit of his former connection with Mary.

As early as 1893, mediums were telling Balfour of messages they were receiving for him from a spirit identifying herself as "the Palm Maiden." Unfortunately, the man was confused, not comforted, by these messages. He had no idea who this was spirit was. Although he felt that he still hadn't contacted his beloved, Arthur Balfour maintained his interest in the "other world." Then, at a séance in 1901, when a message included a reference to "King Arthur," the politician finally realized that his true love *was* trying to contact him. Only then did the moniker "Palm Maiden" make sense to him, for a palm tree was an important symbol on his family's coat of arms.

From 1902 to 1905, Balfour was too busy to indulge in Spiritualism. He had been elected prime minister of Britain. By 1908, however, he was once again able to get in touch with Mary's spirit. She told him in one of her messages that she had remained as faithful to him as he had to her.

Remarkably, this love affair between the world of the living and the world of the dead continued until Arthur James Balfour drew his last breath in 1930, at the age of 82. One can only hope that Mary Lyttleton was there to greet him on the other side.

Murder Not Magic

What could be more romantic than a wedding in a castle? Imagine the castle owner, a baron, walking arm-in-arm with his daughter, the beautiful bride, followed by half a dozen pretty attendants in matching dresses. Why, it would be just like a dream, wouldn't it? Sadly, for *this* bride, Abigail Featherston, her dream wedding became a deadly nightmare.

It wasn't that Abigail hadn't been anxious to get married. As a matter of fact, she wanted that very badly. Unfortunately, her father, the wealthy and powerful baron, disapproved of the man she had chosen. Her intended was handsome enough, but he was poor and had no prospects of bettering his station in life.

Just days after the baron realized that his daughter was about to throw her future away by marrying a simple peasant, the father chose his own future son-in-law—a much more suitable groom, or so the selfish baron thought. To ensure that Abigail did not do anything regrettable, the baron ordered his daughter's true love out of the district with strict orders never to return.

Then, despite Abigail's tearful entreaties, the baron set about planning a grand wedding, complete with a feast the likes of which had not been enjoyed for many a year.

When Abigail met the man she was to wed, the poor woman was heartsick. The man was sickly looking, with poor posture, bad teeth and an offensive body odor. Worse, when he began to speak, Abigail realized that he was about as exciting as yesterday's porridge. She was devastated, especially as she knew her father all too well—he would have his way over any objections she could pose.

Not many weeks later, the wedding day dawned fair and sunny. Invited guests flocked to the castle, the bridal party fussed over last-minute details, and the bride looked lovely—because her veil was covering her face and hiding her tears! When the ceremony was over, the baron instructed everyone to enjoy walks and rides around the castle's beautifully landscaped grounds while he supervised preparation of the banquet.

Once the tables in the castle's dining hall were groaning under the weight of hundreds of huge platters of food, the baron stepped outside to call his guests in for dinner. But no one answered his call. The carefully manicured lawns and gardens surrounding his huge home were empty. There wasn't a soul to be seen anywhere. Thinking the people were being impossibly rude, the baron stormed back into the castle to wait for his inconsiderate daughter and equally inconsiderate guests to return from their excursion.

As the shadows of day lengthened, however, the baron's anger turned to worry. By the time it was completely dark outside, the man was frantic and organized his servants to search for the missing people. Thankfully, he soon heard a cry that warmed his heart: "They're here at last, sire! See, the bride and her party are all walking toward us. They're just over that rise! They'll be sitting down to their meal in just a few moments."

The baron's relief was all-encompassing, but, so as not to admit he'd been worried, the man simply walked into the castle, seated himself and waited for the others to join him. After bowing his head to say a heartfelt prayer of thanksgiving for the safe return of his daughter, the man looked up and smiled. Everyone who had been missing was now seated comfortably at either side of the huge dining table. His soul brimming with relief and joy, the baron stood to propose a toast.

But that was when he noticed that something was wrong—very wrong. Everyone seated around him, even his daughter, was completely, eerily silent. He stared in disbelief at the ghastly faces surrounding him—each and every one of which was streaked with blood. The man rubbed his eyes and shook his head in a vain attempt to clear the horrible image before him. The unseeing eyes of his family and friends continued to stare blankly back at him.

The baron fainted.

As the servants rushed to their master's aid, a gust of chill wind swirled through the room. By the time his staff revived the baron, the apparitions that had frightened him were gone. The father of the bride was alone with his servants in the castle dining hall.

A search for the missing people began the next morning. There wasn't much of a delay before a sad report made its way back to the baron in his castle. The group had been massacred, and their bodies lay in a nearby glen.

No one was ever charged with the mass murder, but some people blamed Abigail's true love. It was whispered that he had gone insane after having been rejected. Some said that he had assembled his friends and together they had murdered the entire wedding party. Then he had killed himself. His body was found among those of the wedding party and guests.

This bloodthirsty legend is so well accepted in the folklore of the Northumberland area of England that there is even a little poem warning of the consequences from the tragic event:

> Still from the rocks at Pinkyncleugh
> The blood of the murdered flows anew;
> And that of the murderer drops alone
> Into the pool 'neath the Raven's stone.

Incredibly, the ending of this story is even more ghoulish than that! It is said that on the anniversary of the tragic wedding, ghostly images of the bride and groom can still be seen making their way to Featherston Castle and their ghoulish wedding feast of death.

The Haunted District

Ye Olde Cock Tavern, the George and Vulture, Bunch of Grapes, Plumbers Arms, Old Cheshire Cheese, the Dog and Duck, Widow's Son, Dirty Dick's—English pubs can have the most interesting names. Sometimes one can only guess (and then shudder!) at the origins of those names. Other times a seemingly strange name can be readily explained. The Hare and Billet, for instance, is on Hare and Billet Road—simple, unless you ever wonder how Hare and Billet Road came by its name—or its ghost.

For nearly 200 years, witnesses have seen the forlorn-looking specter of a woman walking along the oddly named roadway. Everyone who has seen her image reports that the pathetic wraith seems extremely distressed. The revenant is said to be that of an aristocratic woman who, in life, had the bad fortune to fall in love with a cad—worse, a married cad. The man promised that he would leave his wife and asked his lover to meet him by a huge elm tree that once stood on Hare and Billet Road. The woman obeyed her lover's request. She waited there, by the tree, for hours and hours. Her wait was in vain. Finally, she could wait no longer. Her heart broken, the woman fashioned a noose, threw it over one of the elm tree's branches and hanged herself. Sadly, even death didn't bring relief to the tormented woman, as her dreadfully unhappy ghost was reported as recently as 2004.

Just a few blocks away, there was once another lovelorn ghost. Annie Hawkins' equally pathetic soul used to be seen gliding just above a semicircular strip of roadway called the Paragon. It is said that Annie drowned herself in a pond after her love affair ended badly. As her specter has not been seen for decades now, perhaps her soul is finally at rest.

Yet another haunting in the area is tied to the history of Charlton House, a history that goes back nearly 400 years. Sir Adam Newton built the mansion and lived in it until his death, when ownership of the grand old place passed to his son. By the late 1600s, Sir William Langhorne owned Charlton House. His fondest wish was apparently to do as Newton had done and leave the place to his son. Unfortunately, Sir William had no heirs.

When Langhorne's apparently infertile wife died, the man was already in his eighties. The combination of his advanced age and newly changed marital status should probably have been enough to tamp out the man's desire to father a child, but that was not the case. He soon married again—and his new bride was all of 17 years of age! Unfortunately, even this extreme move didn't give Langhorne the heir he so wanted, and his new bride was left a widow after just two months. Yet the man's amorous urges apparently did not die with him. Although there are no reports of sightings, Langhorne's ghost is recognized by his amorous actions and by the fact that he obviously loves the ladies.

Many women staying at Charlton House have been victims of his ghostly presence. Some reported watching and listening in horror as the bedroom door handle turned when they thought they were resting in complete privacy. When they jumped up to ward off their apparent intruder, they found the hallway outside their door empty. Other ladies visiting the house have felt an invisible hand on their derrieres as they made their way up a staircase. It is presumed that the dirty old ghost is still searching for a way to conceive an heir to whom he could leave Charlton House.

This ghost story ends with a sadly ironic twist. A wing of the grand old mansion was damaged by a bomb during World War II. During the repair work that followed, a mummified corpse was discovered hidden in a chimney. It was the body of an infant. No one has ever come forward to solve the mystery of that grisly find in the home of a man who seems to eternally want to father a child.

All three of the hauntings described above are in an area in the southeast of London called Blackheath. The name was likely derived from the words "bleak heath," which apparently captured the essence of the unattractive area when it was named. It is also where the bodies of many plague victims were unceremoniously disposed of during the 14th century, when the Black Death ripped through Europe and England. If it is true, as some students of the paranormal believe, that ghosts are attracted to haunted places, then Blackheath comes by its lovesick ghosts honestly.

Two Ageless Ghostly Love Stories

Ghost stories, like love stories, pepper the history of every culture of the world. Not surprisingly, these tales usually reflect their time and place. Stories from maritime regions, for instance, often involve tragic shipwrecks. The British Isles are full of castles haunted by heartbroken wraiths. Modern roadways, so important to contemporary society, often have sad, ghostly tales associated with them.

The ghosts haunting the folklore of ancient Japan are also distinct—in a rather gruesome way. Those spirits are often angry, bitter and destructive, especially when they involve love affairs that have gone fatally awry. This theme was even built into an entire genre of plays in which the plot would commonly include an illicit love affair followed by the lovers' suicide, with their souls then returning to the earthly plane. In a unique twist, however, these ghosts were eternally tied together with a rope around their waists!

One such tale, which by the early 1800s had become a popular play, involved the eternal triangle of a wronged husband, his unfaithful wife and her determined lover. In order to free his love from her cold and uncaring husband, the lover murdered the husband. Although the dastardly deed apparently went unpunished in this world, as soon as the lovers married, the murdered husband's spirit returned to earth to torment them. Terrified by the haunting, the couple sought protection from the vengeful spirit by means of potions and incantations. But nothing would exorcise the spirit, and before long the immoral pair had also died, presumably joining the murdered husband's vindictive soul in the afterlife where, perhaps, they were eternally tormented.

Another Japanese story tells of a widow who, in her mourning, had become a religious recluse—until her deceased husband's brother attracted her attention and wooed her away from her sanctuary. The pair tried to keep their affair a secret, but soon two servants discovered the truth. The lovers, afraid their secret would soon become common knowledge, silenced the servants in a very permanent way. It would seem that in this instance, too, the murderers went unpunished by the living, but again, the ghosts of their victims returned to haunt and harass them as punishment for their immoral deeds.

A Father's Loving Devotion

Ironically, some of the world's most profound and moving love stories have come from times of war. Of course, romance becomes especially urgent with the threat of a foreshortened future, but war-related love stories are not just of the romantic sort. The horrors of war can thrust people into extraordinary circumstances, heightening their energies and possibly leading them into situations that they would not otherwise have encountered in their lives. The following story is an example of such an incident. It is also an extremely intriguing ghost story.

By early fall of 1939, World War II had begun. Hitler was inciting fear and tension throughout Europe. The Gattones, an Italian family of trapeze artists, were in Berlin at that time to perform at a huge annual festival. For them, the war was a highly personal event because, although Benno Gattone was Italian, his wife, Helenka, was Polish. Italy was an ally of Germany, but Warsaw, the capital city of Poland, had just been invaded and captured by the Germans. Worse, Helenka was, by her very nature, an outspoken woman. She was told time and time again to be careful expressing her anti-Nazi feelings, especially in Germany. Despite the warnings, the woman continued making her feelings known. On September 10, just days before her family's acrobatic act was scheduled to be performed, Helenka was arrested by the Gestapo.

Frantic, Benno left his two younger children in the care of their older brother, 16-year-old Georgio, and went to search for his wife. Neither parent was ever seen alive again. Although they did not know it yet, the children were now orphans, stranded in a strange country with war all around them.

When the day came for the Gattones' performance, young Georgio took his father's place on the trapeze. He knew the family act well enough. He also knew that he was not as accomplished a performer as his father had been, and so he asked to have a safety net strung below the trapezes. The festival manager looked stricken when he heard the boy's request.

"Members of the Gestapo will be in the audience this evening," the man explained. "They were expecting to see the act done without a net. Perhaps we should cancel the performance entirely."

But Georgio wouldn't hear of it. His father had never canceled a show in his entire career, and the boy felt that doing so would be an insult to the older man's reputation.

"All right, then," the youngster agreed. "No net."

That evening, as the show progressed, Georgio was performing exquisitely. All the high-wire tricks had gone well. Georgio was feeling very confident as he approached the hardest maneuver of the trapeze routine. He hurled himself away from his trapeze and flew through the air toward the arms of his father's partner on another trapeze. The man's arms were extended to grasp the boy's hands as Georgio sailed toward him, but something went wrong—dreadfully wrong. Seconds later, the boy was plummeting toward the cement floor beneath—toward certain death.

The audience gasped in horror.

Then, as though propelled by some magical force, another trapeze, one just below the highest apparatus, swung out toward Georgio. Could he grab it in time?

He did.

Tragedy had been averted—but how? How had that empty trapeze moved into the boy's path at the exact second that it was so desperately needed?

Only one aerialist—The Great Gattone—had timing that accurate. The power of the man's love for his son had, in that split second, cheated death.

It wasn't until after the show ended that night that Georgio Gattone and his younger brother and sister learned that their parents had been killed by the Nazis.

As a postscript to this poignant story of loving protection from beyond, it is interesting to note that none of the Gattone children ever performed the trapeze act again.

Manresa Castle

Castles are places we usually associate with Europe and the United Kingdom—not with the United States, and especially not with a workaday place such as Port Townsend in Washington State. Nevertheless, that is exactly where we find the very haunted Manresa Castle. Best of all, ghost hunters are welcome to visit this castle, because it is now an elegant inn.

In September 2004, partly in the name of research but mostly for the challenge of a good ghost hunt, my daughter Deborah and I spent a night in the beautifully restored old building. When we arrived in Port Townsend, we searched our unfamiliar surroundings for the haunted inn we had traveled so far to enjoy—surely a castle would not be hard to spot in a community of normal-sized homes. Our scanning was soon rewarded. There, towering above the landscape, was a turret! You certainly don't have to be English or European to know that where there's a turret, there's a castle. Eager to investigate this western American anomaly, we hurried in the appropriate direction. A few steps later, on a high point of land, we saw the entire imposing Manresa Castle.

Checking in was an experience in time travel. Charles Eisenbeis, who built the castle in the late 19th century as his family's opulent, palatial residence, would no doubt be amazed by the existence of computers in his former home, but he'd have to know that a century-plus of progress has taken place since the building was new.

Eisenbeis emigrated from Prussia in 1856 to make his fortune in the New World. Just a few years later he was a wealthy business owner in Port Townsend. By 1865, Eisenbeis had married an expatriate from his homeland. Soon the young

Manresa Castle

couple had been blessed with four children. Given the family's tremendous affluence and their European heritage, it isn't a surprise that by 1892, Charles had built an enormous home for his family. Perhaps not one given to understatement, the newly successful man called the 30-room house Eisenbeis Castle.

By the time his wife died in 1880, Charles had become the town's first mayor. Soon he married again. Over time, Eisenbeis and his second wife, Kate, added four more children to the family. Charles died in 1902, at the age of 70, having truly realized the dream he had come to America to pursue. A few years after Charles' death, Kate remarried and left the castle, which stood empty, except for the resident caretaker, until the late 1920s. In that same decade, by coincidence, the beautiful old building first became haunted.

It's believed that the forlorn spirit's name is Kate, although this could simply be a confusion with the name of Eisenbeis's second wife. Be that as it may, the young woman now known as Kate had made arrangements to stay at the castle until the man she loved and was engaged to marry returned from sea. For days Kate sat with eager anticipation, looking out the window of a corner bedroom. Days turned to weeks but still she stayed at her post. No one could persuade her to break her vigil. And that was where the messenger found her when the tragic news finally made its way to the mainland. The young woman's fiancé had been lost at sea.

Utterly heartbroken, the girl threw herself out the window and to her death nearly four stories below.

If Kate's suicide was an attempt to join her beloved in his afterlife, it is unlikely that she was successful, for her soul has apparently never left the realm of the castle. It has long been said that her ghost haunts the place—especially room 306, which had been her world for those agonizingly long weeks and the place where she flung herself from this world to the next.

Not long after that terrible tragedy, Eisenbeis Castle was put up for sale. Even though few people knew about Kate's suicide, no one wanted to buy the place. Not only was it far too big for most people's purposes, the upkeep on such a mansion was considerably more expensive than most were willing, or able, to pay. While the building stood eerily empty, its windows stared like lifeless eyes down over the town, mocking the pride Charles Eisenbeis had felt when he built the enormous place.

In 1928 new owners were found. An order of Jesuit priests decided that the castle would make an excellent training facility. They not only purchased Eisenbeis Castle but also set to work building a new wing with 20 additional residence rooms. The religious order named their new academy Manresa Hall in honor of the place in Spain where their founder, St. Ignatius, had his spiritual awakening.

Legend has it that during this time there was yet another suicide in the building. The story goes that a priest hanged himself in the attic, directly under the castle's turret. Some people dispute the veracity of this story, but others swear to having seen his ghostly image forever suspended from the aging rafters. That debate aside, Manresa Hall, the Jesuit training facility, remained in Port Townsend until 1968, when the religious order moved its quarters to Seattle.

The building was empty again—and even larger than it had been the first time the property changed hands.

Fortunately, this unique piece of American history was saved from the wrecker's ball by a couple who envisioned a future for the enormous old structure. After investing countless hours of backbreaking labor reviving the huge and very rundown building, they opened their elegant inn and named the place Manresa Castle—in honor of its two previous incarnations.

Since then, Manresa Castle has changed hands twice and has earned a reputation as an exceptional hostelry with a world-class dining room. It has also become acknowledged as an extremely haunted place—so haunted that, several years ago, management began inviting guests to note their ghostly encounters in special log books that the hotel kept.

For a while, the manager left those log books in rooms 302 and 306, the two most haunted rooms. After a while,

Ghost hunters book months in advance to make sure they can stay in the most haunted room at Manresa Castle.

though, they noticed that an inconvenient pattern had developed. Frequently, within an hour of the time guests checked in to either of those rooms, the folks would ask to be moved to another suite. Of course, the hotel staff always obliged the request. Eventually they ascertained that the guests had become uncomfortable after reading the descriptions of the hauntings detailed in the log books. Sensibly, the hotel executives then moved the books to the administration office so that guests would see them only if they wished to.

Sadly, not even that plan proved to be a perfect solution because several log books, with long and painstakingly detailed notations about guests' encounters with the phantoms, have been released for guests' perusal and have not been returned. While that is undeniably a great loss to the records of Manresa Castle, the larger concern should be for the person or persons who took them. It is generally accepted that stealing creates bad karma for an individual; it's scary to think what stealing records of otherworldly activities might create! Despite the thefts, there are still dozens of remaining notebooks filled with the particulars of people's inexplicable experiences in this haunted hotel.

The ghost of the priest is not a very public specter because his soul usually stays in the attic, where the man apparently took his life. Fewer people have seen his image because that area of Manresa Castle isn't open to guests. Kate's spirit, however, is much more available to visitors— including my daughter and me! Not long after we arrived we were shown to our room—the very haunted room 306, as requested. Ron Myhre, general manager, and Lyle Ruskin, a member of the castle's front desk staff, then generously spent time showing us around and revealing details of the latest encounters with the grieving soul of Kate.

Just two months before our arrival, a family consisting of mother Lori, father Mark, teenage daughter Chelsea and teenage son James checked in to the castle and were shown to their rooms on the third floor. Lori later noted that the family had spent a "delightful" evening and specified that nothing out of the ordinary had occurred. The next morning was an entirely different matter. Lori explained, "James went to use the restroom (room 303) down the hall and came back concerned that he had heard a woman crying mournfully in the bathroom marked 305, but the lights were out in that room."

Convinced that someone was in distress, young James asked his father to accompany him back to that bathroom door. Mark also heard the sobs. Because the sounds were so clearly those of a woman, he didn't go into the room himself and asked Lori to investigate instead.

Lori wrote, "By the time I got there she was no longer crying. I did, however, hear movement coming from inside the room."

Not wanting to take the chance of invading someone's privacy at a difficult time, Lori knocked on the door and "asked if someone in there needed help."

The apparent answer came in the form of two knocks on the inside of the door.

"At that point, we decided to call the front desk to tell them what was going on," Lori noted. "They sent up four maids to check the situation out. When the maids opened the door, it was dark inside and no one was in there."

That didn't ease anyone's mind because tissues "had been strewn about" the room. It looked much as you'd imagine a room might look after someone had been using tissues while crying.

"We had never left the door unattended since Mark and James had heard the crying, so no one could have left without us seeing," Lori explained.

Hoping to find a rational explanation for the disturbing sounds, Lori suggested that perhaps the sobbing had not actually come from the bathroom but from the room next to it. "While we were out in the hall discussing this possibility, a man came out of the nearby room. He had his keys in his hand, ready to check out. We told him of the crying, but he

One of the windows that is said to be the one Kate jumped from.

knew nothing of it. After he left we looked in the bathroom of that room but there was nobody there."

The mystery was far from being solved.

"By then, daughter Chelsea was getting ready for the day in the bathroom (303) when the crying started again. Three members of our family had now heard this crying and again movement was heard coming from bathroom 305."

Despite their strange experiences, possibly with the after-life, the family's lives had to go on. "We were excited by the encounters with the unknown, but oddly none of us felt frightened. We felt a sense of disbelief...there was no logical explanation for our experiences."

As planned, the family checked out of Manresa Castle, but were clearly not able to put the inexplicable events behind them.

"We had business that was to bring us back to Port Townsend in a couple of weeks, so we booked room 302 for one night and room 306 for the second."

They knew that these were the two most haunted rooms in the hotel. Room 302 is directly below the turret where the priest ended his life, and one of the windows in room 306 is said to be the one Kate jumped from. Despite this history, Lori explained that they were really more interested in the Bradbury and Bradbury wallpapers the rooms were deco-rated with than they were the spirits! She explained, "We were going to paper our house soon with paper from this company and we thought that spending time in the rooms would help us choose the design we wanted."

The family once again checked into Manresa Castle, but this time they went straight to bed for the night. Mother, father and two children had already fallen asleep in room 302 "when Chelsea was awakened by a spooky feeling." The girl opened her eyes and saw "the silhouette of a hand reaching over her. She then saw what looked to her like a man wearing long, flowing robes hovering over her bed."

After that initial sighting, both mother and daughter "were awakened repeatedly throughout the night by a very cold and damp presence startling" them. "This time, we were scared," Lori penned.

Scared or not, the family stuck to the plan to spend a second night at Manresa Castle; this one in the room that Kate's spirit is believed to haunt.

"We were watching television when, around midnight, we noticed that someone had strewn unused tissues all over the [en suite] bathroom floor. This seemed very spooky to us because of our previous experience with Kate and the tissues. We repeatedly questioned each other and nobody in our family had used tissues at all that evening. We felt that Kate had remembered us and found a way to communicate that to us."

Even if they were just intending to view different wallpapers, the ghostly interactions that seemed to go along with the interior decorating were taking their toll.

"We had not slept well the night before in room 302 and weren't feeling up to another night of ghostly encounters. Chelsea seemed particularly sensitive to Kate and was strongly feeling her presence," Lori wrote. The girl knew she'd had more than enough of haunted rooms when she felt her back being scratched when no one visible was near her. Sure of what she'd felt, the girl asked her mother to look at her back. Lori "checked and was able to see small scratch marks."

Minutes later the family was moved to a quiet room on the second floor where they "passed the remainder of our stay uneventfully."

The thoughtful family concluded their notes by writing, "None of us have ever had any experiences with ghosts before though we were open to the possibility that they exist. We never thought when we came to Manresa Castle that we would experience the supernatural things that we did. Though both Lori and Chelsea have always had occasional premonitions and a high level of—I don't know—percep- tiveness—we wonder—why us?"

Less than two months after Lori left her insightful and philosophical wonderings, another guest, a woman named Jerry, noted that this was her second visit to the castle. She wrote that "the service and the people are really great and the food is some of the best we have encountered in our many travels." Then she began to explain her *real* reason for adding to the log book. She had seen her roommate go into the bathroom alone, but "when she came out [Jerry] saw some- one else behind her helping her get back to her bed…"

This sighting was clear enough that Jerry was able to describe the image accompanying her friend and firmly maintained that she had seen "a tall woman in a white gown behind Linda." In her own defense, Jerry noted, "I don't do sleeping pills or anything else at night! I know what I saw!"

And up to the time of our stay at Manresa Castle, those were the most recent notations about ghostly encounters at the haunted inn.

If you would love to see this unique piece of architecture, but don't want to encounter either of the ghosts in the castle, you simply have to stay on one of the first two floors. However, if you are brave, you might ask for a look into the attic, where you might see the image of the priest. If you have a romantic and slightly curious nature, do stay in room 306, where the long-dead Kate's heartbroken soul has remained for more than 80 years.

Disappointingly, Kate did not show herself to either my daughter or me, although as we explored one of the elegantly paneled hallways, we did encounter a strange pocket of intensely cold air that vanished as soon as we mentioned it. Oh, and then there was that "something" that I was positive followed me down the steep, creaking staircase from the haunted third floor. But we were not discouraged. We'll be back to visit Manresa Castle again, and perhaps then we'll have a face-to-face encounter with Kate of the Haunted Heart!

BIBLIOGRAPHY

Adams, Charles J. III. *New York City Ghost Stories.* Reading, PA: Exeter House Books, 1996.

Alexander, John. *Ghosts: Washington's Most Famous Ghost Stories.* Arlington, VA: Washington Book Trading Company, 1988.

Blundell, Nigel and Roger Boar. *The World's Greatest Ghost.* London: Octopus Books, 1983.

Brooks, J.A. *Ghosts and Legends of Wales.* Norwold, Wales: Jarrold Publishing, 1987.

Chambers, Aidan. *Great British Ghosts.* London: Pan Books, 1974.

Christensen, Jo-Anne. *Ghost Stories of Saskatchewan.* Toronto: Hounslow Press, 1995.

Fate, June 1974.

Holzer, Hans. *Travel Guide to Haunted Houses.* New York: Black Dog and Leventhal Publishers, 1998.
———. *Window to the Past: Exploring History Through ESP.* Richmond Hill, ON: Simon & Schuster, 1970.

Hurwood, Bernard J. *Ghosts, Ghouls and Other Horrors.* New York: Scholastic Book Services, 1974.
———. *Haunted Houses.* New York: Scholastic Book Services, 1972.

Jessome, Bill. *More Maritime Mysteries.* Halifax, NS: Nimbus Publishing, 2001.

Jones, Richard. *Haunted London.* London: New Holland Publishers, 2004.

Kermeen, Frances. *Ghostly Encounters.* New York: Warner Books, 2002.

Klein, Victor E. *New Orleans Ghosts.* Metairie, LA: Lycanthrope Press, 1996.

Macklin, John. *The Enigma of the Unknown.* New York: Ace Books, 1967.
———. *Strange Encounters.* New York: Ace Books, 1968.

Moore, R. *Sussex Ghosts*. St. Ives, Cornwall, England: James Pike, 1976.

O'Ryan, Bridie. "Irish Widow's Ghost is a Phantom Hitchhiker." *Beyond,* April 1969.

Phantom Encounters. Alexandria, VA: Time-Life Books, 1988.

Raybin Emert, Phyllis. *Frightening Phantoms and Haunted Habitats*. New York: Tom Doherty Associates, 1996.

Saltzman, Pauline. *Ghosts and Other Strangers*. New York: Lancer Books, 1970.
———. *Strange Spirits*. New York: Paperback Library, 1967.
———. *The Strange and the Supernatural*. New York: Paperback Library, 1968.

Scott, Beth and Michael Norman. *Haunted Heartland*. New York: Warner Books, 1985.

Skinner, Charles M. *Myths and Legends of Our Own Land*. New York: L.P. Lippincott Company, 1896.

Sleman, Tom. *Haunted Liverpool 3*. Liverpool: The Bluecoat Press, 1998.

Smith, Warren. *Strange Hexes*. New York: Popular Library, 1970.

Spencer, John and Anne. *The Encyclopedia of Ghosts and Spirits, Volume 2*. London: Headline Book Publishing Company, 2001.

Stonehouse, Frederick. *Haunted Lake*. Duluth, MN: Lake Superior Port Cities, Inc., 1997.

Tralins, Robert. *The Hidden Spectre*. New York: Avon Books, 1970.

Zepke, Terrance. *Ghosts of the Carolina Coasts*. Sarasota, FL: Pineapple Press, 1999.

**GHOST
HOUSE**

ADD TO YOUR GHOST HOUSE COLLECTION
WITH THESE NEW TITLES FULL OF
FASCINATING MYSTERIES AND TERRIFYING TALES

ROMANTIC GHOST STORIES

by Julie Burtinshaw

Based on true accounts, these stories explore lovers united in death, the lasting effects of a lost love among the living and the tempestuous infidelities whose painful consequences never fade away. A pensive spirit continues to wander a grand old hotel on the Pacific coast, still celebrating the married bliss that was shattered by an international scandal. After her fiancé is killed, a Colorado woman abandons all will to live, but her spirit returns to a frontier stagecoach station as the "Gray Lady." These stories and more in *Romantic Ghost Stories*.

$10.95USD/$14.95CDN • ISBN10: 1-894877-28-4/ISBN13: 978-1-894877-28-2
5.25" x 8.25" • 224 pages

FAMOUS PEOPLE OF THE PARANORMAL

by Chris Wangler

Shamans, psychics, yogis, channelers—almost every culture singles out people with extraordinary gifts. This ambitious book explores the bizarre lives of paranormal celebrities through the ages. As you might imagine, not everyone in this unusual field is genuine; author Chris Wangler also exposes a handful of bona fide paranormal charlatans.

$10.95USD/$14.95CDN • ISBN10: 1-894877-28-4/ISBN13: 978-1-894877-28-2
5.25" x 8.25" • 240 pages

NEW APRIL 2006

GHOSTS FROM AROUND THE WORLD

by Susan Smitten

Ghosts, it seems, are everywhere, even in corners of the world where you'd least expect them. In this new collection, ghost story expert Susan Smitten leaves no stone unturned in her quest for proof of hauntings. Smitten has interviewed eyewitnesses in places such as Ireland, Japan, South Africa and Germany, discovering that while geography and history may vary greatly, ghost motives for returning after death are remarkably consistent.

$10.95USD/$14.95CDN • ISBN10: 1-894877-65-9/ISBN13: 978-1-894877-65-7
5.25" x 8.25" • 224 pages

These and many more Ghost House books are available from your local bookseller or by ordering direct. U.S. readers call 1-800-518-3541. In Canada, call 1-800-661-9017.